1980s Kid

by Jade Heasley

God bless,

Jade Heasley

Please note: Barbie® and Barbie® dolls are all
registered trademarks of Mattel, Inc.

Published by CreateSpace

Dedication

To Mom:

Thank you for all of your love and support that you've given me. You've taught me about faith, hope, and love. You taught me to read and write (skills that came in very handy while writing this book), and how to appreciate family, humor, education, antiques, and rock-and-roll. You always made me feel that I was creative and unique and had something special to offer the world.

To Dad:

Thank you for all of your hard work to support our family over the years, and for all the camping trips, boat rides, and hikes. I especially thank you for your continued support in my grown-up pursuits and for keeping my car running like new.

To Seth:

My only sibling and partner in bratty pranks, we've shared a lot of laughter over the years, haven't we? Thank you for helping to make my childhood so much fun.

In Loving Memory of Dorothy A. (Wertz) Harman

My Gram loved me, encouraged me, befriended me, and made me a big priority. She brought an immeasurable amount of good into my life. She also wrote a column in a local newspaper for nearly twenty years that really inspired me in my own writing endeavors.

To the Family of Dorothy A. (Wertz) Harman

To my Mom's extended family, all of my aunts, uncles, cousins, and my amazing nieces, you have always been there and have all helped shape me into the person I am today. I thank you that I can count on your love and support always. You have helped me to sharpen my wit and added a lot of fun and value to my life. Our family get-togethers have been responsible for some of my happiest memories – especially when we're playing Trivial Pursuit and eating way too much junk.

To my Dad's extended family:

To Grammy and Poppy, Papa and Grandma Deb, Grandma Annette and Grandpa Aronne, and my aunts, uncles and cousins, thank you for the love and support you have given me.

The Time Warp

       I was standing in the living room scrolling through the music videos on my iPod and had just downloaded Bon Jovi's "Runaway." I was happy that iTunes had added some more of the classic 1980s Bon Jovi videos to their inventory, but then I was struck by just how far technology had come in the last few decades. I was holding my iPod in the palm of my hand watching the video I had first seen as a preschooler and was suddenly struck with an odd feeling that I was caught in some sort of time warp. I felt like I was being pulled backward into a drastically different but strangely familiar world that I had not been to in a very long time. I was no longer a twenty-something enjoying awesome, retro rock-and-roll on modern technology; I was a child in the 1980s glancing into an amazing future where you could have a color TV, VCR, and command over MTV in the palm of your hand. It was incredible! But a moment later I was an adult again, longing for the care free days of childhood rather than the quarter life crisis of student loan debt and having to pay a small fortune for a tank of gasoline. I am open to the possibility that the "time warp" feeling that came as quickly and unexpectedly as lightning might have been a side effect of the migraine headaches I suffer from. But that's all the more reason I wanted to revisit my childhood – migraine headaches weren't invented until after the 1980s drew to a close (at least in my experience).

For days afterward my mind kept drifting back to that feeling of amazement over just how far and how fast technology had developed and the "time warp" feeling that I had experienced, but even more so to the 1980s. Back when everything was radical and everyone, at one point or another, walked like an Egyptian. It was a time when rock stars wore fluffy, permed mullets and spandex leggings but still managed to look cool. It was back when Bill Cosby sold pudding by day and got phenomenal primetime ratings at night. Pee-Wee Herman may not have been the King of Cartoons but no one could deny he ruled Saturday morning. Every cool kid had a metal TV tray at home and a metal lunch box at school. MTV and VH1 played nothing but music videos. McDonald's sold their food in Styrofoam containers. It was when Marty McFly playing "Johnny B. Goode" at the Enchantment Under the Sea dance was the coolest thing that you had ever seen, and made you want to learn the electric guitar. This was back when John Hughes was the king of the box office and if Emilio Estevez, Judd Nelson, Alley Sheedy, Molly Ringwald, and Anthony Michael Hall attended your school you would have done everything in your power to get Saturday detention. VCRs, Walkmans, and home computer systems were recognized as the ultimate status symbols of the American middle class. Michael J. Fox was selling Diet Pepsi and Max Headroom was selling Coke. Almost every cereal box had a cool prize, and more sugar than essential vitamins. Every store, restaurant, and street corner had a pay phone. AT&T and MCI were doing battle for control of your phone line. Gasoline cost 93¢ a gallon. Boom boxes and break dancing were awesome. *The Boy Who Could Fly* debuted and will always remain one of the greatest fantasy movies of all time. It was when every kid in America was a devoted fan of Nickelodeon and longed to win the Super Toy Run Sweepstakes and be a contestant on *Double Dare*. Most department stores in America sold lawn darts (aka "Jarts") and many people spent countless lovely afternoons sailing the occasionally lethal projectiles through the air. This was when Reese's Pieces were purchased by little kids anxious to eat them as a snack and to use them as bait for extra-terrestrials. You had at least one school picture taken that was a "dual image" photograph, and the pictures taken at home meant waiting five minutes for the gray Polaroid image to clear so you could see the results. Eventually your parents probably switched to a 110 camera which required a flip flash, until they got a more advanced 110 camera that had the flash built right in.

It was an era of Peter Billingsly selling Hershey's Chocolate Syrup and longing for a Red Ryder BB gun in *A Christmas Story*, one of the greatest Christmas movies ever made. It was a time of wearing leg warmers while you were walking on sunshine. We learned that UFOs were capable of time travel by watching *Flight of the Navigator*. It was when all the cool kids at the arcade had big teased up hair, Jordache jeans, huge baggy t-shirts, and Swatch Watches. If it was winter you were wearing an oversized sweater with shoulder pads that were eight inches thick. It was an era of wearing three pairs of socks over your pegged pants and walking around in L.A. Gear High Tops; but of course the reason we wore our socks *over* our pant legs was because our stonewashed jeans were too skin tight to leave room for socks. Looking back at the photos the fashions may seem ridiculous but in your heart of hearts you know everything about that decade was cool (except maybe mullets and rattails, but you could get away with them then). You have probably wished you could return to that era and may have even attempted to build your own Flux Capacitor. Everyone who lived during the 1980s, especially those of us who were young, knows that it was a truly awesome decade.

If you are a true fan of the 1980s you know that "Video Killed the Radio Star" by The Buggles was the first music video ever played on MTV. You know that Toni Basil was in her 40s when she did the video for "Mickey." You are also well aware that before Patrick Swayze and Jennifer Grey were cutting the rug at Kellerman's they were killing communists in Colorado. You know that *The Breakfast Club* and *Some Kind of Wonderful* were the best John Hughes movies of the decade, and arguably the best of his career. You recognize that Activision was responsible for creating some of the best video games of the decade. You remember when Big Wheel tricycles were a big deal, and if you were a kid you clearly remember how tough it was to pedal a bike with hollow plastic wheels down the sidewalk, and you can distinctly remember the loud grating, scraping noise those wheels produced. You also know that if Ralph Macchio would have just unleashed some of those *Karate Kid* moves on those drunken Socs that *The Outsiders* would have had a much happier ending. Poor Ralph! If only the Daniel Larusso role would have come before the Johnny Cade role!

So after several days of reminiscing I have decided to commit some of my own 1980s memories to paper. This isn't intended to be a complete memoir of my childhood; it's just a collection of some of my memories from the 1980s. A complete memoir would probably be somewhat dull to read, you don't want to hear about all the times I was on my best behavior or doing ordinary things like jump roping or coloring in a coloring book. As every adult who was once a child can tell you there is a fine line between behaving and misbehaving and I enjoyed dancing on that line as often as I could, seeing how much I could get away with before I got into trouble. I figured you might like to read about the times that I was being bratty and discovering the new technological wonders of the 1980s, and so I have omitted the boring parts of my childhood from this book because I'm sure you don't want to hear about the times when I was following all the rules. I hope you enjoy my book because if you do we both win. If not, well, you've already purchased the book and I still get the royalties. So I guess I win even if you hate my book, but I have a feeling that you'll like this book almost as much as Mikey liked Life Cereal.

Happy Birthday, Jadie

I was born on August 7, 1980 (it was a Thursday, at 4:07 a.m. if you care to know the *Rain Man* level details). I made my grand debut in State College, Pennsylvania in an area known as Happy Valley. As a child I always assumed that the valley was given that name after I was born in celebration of me, but I was disappointed to learn later in life that the valley was so named before my birth. Yet this minor detail doesn't stop me from attempting to fool gullible people into thinking that the region was formerly called, "The Valley of Gloom and Despair" but was changed to Happy Valley in my honor. Usually I can at least get someone to question me on this point. I have to say that gullible people are almost always fun to talk to.

The origin of my own name, Jade, is something I never joke about because it is such an amazing story. Mom had decided that she was either going to name me Megan or Sarah Elizabeth after her maternal grandmother. Every day Mom read the birth announcements in the paper and noticed that both Megan and Sarah were becoming very common and began to rethink the name choices because she wanted me to have a unique name. With her due date rapidly approaching Mom was trying to come up with a unique name for a baby girl. One day she thought of the name Jade and was struck by it, but was uncertain if she should use it since it was so different. She had never heard the gemstone used as a name before. Shortly after that Mom was talking to her mother, my Gram Harman, on the telephone and Gram said, "You know I was lying in bed last night thinking about names and I thought that Jade would be a really neat name for a little girl." Mom was reeling in shock, she hadn't mentioned to anyone that she was considering using the name Jade. The striking coincidence was not lost on Mom, who thought that it was meant to be and I was given the name Jade Lauren. A few months after I was born we moved to my mother's hometown about an hour away. This is the place that I have always considered my home, and a big reason that I love my little hometown is that nearly everyone in my Mom's big extended family has always lived here too, so we always get together for holidays and birthdays, sports and school activities, and we visit each other often.

Mom was a stay-at-home-mom who doted over me and thought everything I did was cute (well, mostly, I did try her patience from time to time with some creative bratty adventures but that was only when she caught me). Mom has always been cheerful and optimistic, and has a very sweet nature. She spent the days of my childhood teaching me how to read and write, how to spell, and do basic math. She made sure I always had plenty of dolls and a ready supply of coloring books and Crayola Crayons. She read at least one story book to me every day, and she also read to me from my children's Bible on a daily basis. She took me on walks to visit Gram or to go to the playground. One of the best parts about going for a walk was being near the train tracks as a massive train, pulled by a big blue Conrail engine sailed through town. When I was little most trains still had a caboose at the end, and I always waved to the guys onboard and was thrilled when they waved back.

Dad was a hard-working auto mechanic who appreciated practical jokes. He could be strict, but I learned early in life that if he found humor in my endeavors away from careful adherence to the rules I was encouraged rather than disciplined. One time when I was about eight he tried to scare one of my friends by hiding a rubber lizard in her shoe, so I took revenge by hiding a fake centipede and some other toy insects on his pillow. The following night I went to bed and discovered these same critters on my pillow. Not to be outdone, the next night I waited about a half hour before I went to bed and got an ice cube out of the freezer and put it on his pillow. Dad told me the next day he was surprised when he went to bed that half of his face was suddenly immersed in a cold, wet puddle. He congratulated me on my creativity and declared me the winner of the three day prank war; I guess he was fearful of what else my brain could devise at his expense. Victory was especially sweet when I heard him bragging to other grownups about the grand prank-plotting prodigy that his daughter was.

After nearly four years of being an only child I was joined by my brother Seth. I remember Daddy taking me to the hospital and holding me up to the nursery window so I could see the couple of babies in their little bassinets. Daddy told me to pick out which baby brother I wanted. *I got to pick?* I realized that as the firstborn I would have some special privileges but I had no clue that my power extended to the realm of getting to choose my own sibling. I carefully looked at all the babies, and I decided on a particular one. He stood out because his skin had a nice lemony tinge to it (which I later learned was jaundice), but mostly I picked this particular infant because there was just something about him that I liked. Amazingly, the baby I chose really was my brother! I adored my baby brother and felt very proud to be a big sister.

Let me start off with this disclaimer: since I was born in 1980, I don't remember much before 1983. But what I do remember of 1983 was awesome, and considering how young I was, is it any wonder that these early memories occur in short, colorful bursts? It seems that what I remember clearly are big and exciting events, like birthdays and Christmas mornings. My consistent memories of typical days don't start until I was closer to the age of five, so if the early memories I share in the next few paragraphs seem choppy and disconnected it's because that's how I remember them. So if some of this first chapter seems written in a somewhat spastic manner and revolves around toys and birthday cakes, I apologize. But in the spirit of writing truthfully and giving you a window into my early childhood, this is what it is. However, as I grew older and my capacity for remembering ordinary things, as well as my keen powers of observation and a carefully cultivated bratty streak grew the events of my childhood become more interesting. I had debated on whether or not I should include these few recollections, but since they help set the tone for my childhood I decided to keep them in.

I spent many happy birthdays in the 1980s. All of my birthdays were fantastic days because my Mom carefully planned every detail of each of my birthday parties and made sure I had lots of presents. Some of my earliest memories are of my third birthday. My third birthday stands out because my parents got me the best gift that I could ever have imagined: a metal swing set. It was beautiful! It had white metal poles with some of sort geometric design stamped on it in blue and brown, which was very cool for that time. It had a sliding board, a teeter-totter, two swings, and something that I called a "space swing" (I'm not sure why, other than I sometimes used it as a rocket when I played astronaut), which were two bench style swings that faced each other and was big enough to seat four little kids, and a short metal bar that looked like a trapeze type of thing. Unfortunately I was far too clumsy and uncoordinated to use the trapeze swing but I had a lot of fun with the rest of the swing set. Some other awesome gifts I got that year included a real metal wagon from Papa Heasley, a plastic toy stove from my Uncle Jim that included play food, pans, and a green gingham bag to carry everything in that I cleverly used as a table cloth, and Smurf sheets for my big girl bed from my Gram Harman (I loved Smurfs!). I don't remember my birthday cake or any of the games, but I remember the presents which means that I was somewhat caught up in the materialism that would later define the decade.

Another truly classic birthday I can remember was my 5th. I can't imagine that any child in the 1980s had a cooler party than I did that year. It was 1985 and my Mom let me pick out all the paper table wear and party accessories. I went with Cabbage Patch Kids party hats, paper plates, paper table cloths, and hanging garland. My Mom ordered me a cake from her friend whom as a child I referred to as "The Cake Lady." Her baking talent knew no bounds, she could decorate cakes in extraordinary ways and her recipe for icing is the best icing I've ever tasted in my life. For my 5th birthday The Cake Lady made me the coolest cake I had ever seen: Pac-Man. She made Pac-Man out of a round cake pan and covered three-quarters of him in yellow icing. The last quarter of his mouth was covered in chocolate icing, giving the impression that his mouth was open. I had no idea that you could mix white icing and chocolate icing together on the same cake and the levels of The Cake Lady's confectionary genius left me astounded. But as cool as Pac-Man was, the ghosts were awesome. In addition to the cake she had made some cupcakes, but instead of merely icing the tops, she peeled the papers off and iced the whole, entire cupcake and transformed them into the little ghosts just like the ones in the Atari game. It was a great cake.

My presents that year were awesome. Mom and Dad got me the deluxe set of The Heart Family dolls, and the Heart Family Nursery play set, among other things. My beloved Gram Harman got me a Hello Kitty Hello Color doll that was stuffed with a sponge type of material so that you could take it in the swimming pool or bath tub. The best part was that Hello Kitty changed colors when she was submerged in water! No, the doll didn't turn blue to look like she was drowning if that's what you're wondering - her clothes changed color. I loved that doll. Next to the Atari 800 Home Computer System I think she was the most technologically advanced toy I owned up until that point of my life. My Aunt Kelly got me "Fluff," a little white cat for my Barbie® doll that came with a ton of accessories which were totally cool. Fluff even had his own room in my Barbie® doll's house.

Other memorable 1980s birthday cakes included my 6th birthday when I had a Cabbage Patch Kid cake, my 8th birthday cake which had Pee-Wee Herman on it, along with Magic Screen, Chairy and Clocky. Other memorable presents included my seventh birthday when I got a lavender plastic GE boom box that had an AM/FM radio *and* cassette player! It even came with headphones that stayed in a built-in storage space in the back and a three foot antenna. On my eighth birthday I got the Super Dough Snack Shop (the commercial had the coolest jingle) and a Fisher-Price Microscope set.

I hope that everyone can look back at their childhood and have good memories of their birthday parties, but there was just something special about being a kid in the 1980s.

Memories of My Favorite Toys: The Good, the Bad, and the Traumatic

Looking back to Christmas of 1983 I can distinctly remember two moments. One was looking over at my pregnant mother and thinking that next year Santa Claus would be bringing presents to me as well as to my new baby brother or sister. The second is the moment I ripped the wrapping paper off the present that my Uncle Jim had given me and found myself staring in the face of an authentic, genuine Barbie® doll! She must have been as thrilled to see me as I was to see her because she was beaming at me with her big plastic smile. I could scarcely believe it. Barbie® was a toy for big kids! Did that mean that I had somehow crossed the threshold from little kid to big kid overnight? I must have! Uncle Jim seemed to think so and he was really smart so it must have been true. I was a big girl! My Barbie® doll was my favorite present that year. She had blonde hair and blue eyes that were graced with classy, elegant blue eye shadow. She had a bright purple swimming suit, blue plastic sunglasses and a pink beach bag that cleverly unfolded into a beach towel.

My Mom was happy that I gladly welcomed Mattel's greatest achievement into my own inner circle of favorite toys, because Mom's Barbie® doll had been one of her favorite toys when she was a child. It is a strange phenomenon that some men try to live their sports fantasies through their sons by pushing them to excel at sports that they may or may not be interested in. But my Mom saw me playing with my Barbie® dolls and, much to my benefit, must have seen something of herself in me and lived out of all her childhood Barbie® doll dreams through me. She would spend the next several years indulging me by expanding my collection with dolls, cars, clothing, and play sets, telling me how much fun it must be to have all the Barbie® accessories I did because Mattel didn't have nearly as many Barbie® toys in the 1960s as they did now. Looking back she must have spent about $3,000,000 on Barbie® dolls and accessories for me over the years.

The following Christmas when I was four Santa Claus brought me a Barbie® house with a working pink elevator! The house was three stories high and was taller than me! Santa also brought me some furniture for my Barbie® house including beds, bedspreads, pillows, and a magenta velour couch. I was very impressed that one of Santa's elves had made the Barbie® couch a cream colored afghan that was just like the one Mommy had made for the 1980s must have sofa bed that dominated our own living room. Since the previous Christmas my Barbie® collection had grown to include a few more dolls so Santa brought lots of clothes for them.

Over the years my collection continued to grow, and Barbie® was my favorite childhood toy (Lego bricks and the Atari are tied for second place). I later received The Heart Family, a set of dolls that were the same size as

Ken and Barbie® and included two babies. Since they were advertised as "Friends of Barbie" they eventually bought a twenty seven dollar house next to Barbie® and moved in. They had a big blue convertible that had two car seats in the back to protect the babies and seatbelts in the front seats in case of a collision, but Mr. Heart was a safe driver and never had any type of traffic incident.

I didn't have a Ken doll for quite some time but one day between the Christmas of getting Barbie® and the Christmas that I got the Barbie® house we were out of town visiting my great-grandparents, Grammy and Poppy Heasley. During the visit Mom took me to a small store that had a really long aisle of inexpensive toys. The aisle seemed to stretch the whole way to the ceiling! Mom was buying me a toy to reward me for good behavior and told me I could pick any toy I wanted. I wasn't really sure what I wanted, until I looked up on a high shelf and spotted a generic G. I. Joe type of doll. He was twelve inches of pure plastic muscle and stood at attention in his cardboard box and stared out the clear plastic window with his steady eyes, molded brunette hair, camouflage uniform, plastic M16 rifle and other battle accessories. Even though he wasn't Ken, my match making instincts told me that he would be a good man for Barbie®, or at least good enough until I got a real Ken. Barbie® seemed to like, or should I say tolerate, G.I. Joe enough to at least be polite to him and show him a certain level of token courtesy but she and I both knew that she was settling. She was kind enough to call him "G.I. Joe" instead of "Generic G.I. Joe," she cooked him dinner and let him watch baseball on her little pink television. He in return attempted to loosen up his militant ways by learning to play her red plastic electric guitar and by never throwing any grenades or firing his M16 in her house. They had a mediocre relationship for a few years until Christmas Day when I was seven and got a real Ken doll. Finally! A real Ken! He was very handsome with his plastic blonde hair, big muscles, and a great smile that showed off his gleaming white teeth. He was wearing black pants with suspenders and had a shimmering neon orange and yellow t-shirt with a screen printed slice of pizza on it. He even came with white sneakers, a plastic slice of pizza and two miniature cans of soda. Somehow word must have spread from the toys under the Christmas tree up the stairs to my bedroom where all my Barbie® dolls were kept because G.I. Joe mysteriously disappeared. Ken moved into the Barbie® house, but no one ever saw G.I. Joe again.

As time marched on both Barbie® houses eventually became fully furnished. The Heart Family house had no bathroom, but the Barbie® house did. The Heart Family had a powder blue tub that could be filled with water and included a shower head attachment that really squirted water but I ended up giving it to my Barbie® doll since the only place The Heart Family had to keep it at their house was the roof, and that would have been a far too absurd location. The tub wasn't the only Barbie® bath fixture though, because Mattel even made a pink plastic Barbie® toilet that really flushed water and I'm proud to say that I owned one. Unfortunately the toilet didn't come with a sink for her to wash her hands, so I made her wash her hands in the tub. I couldn't let her walk around with unwashed bathroom hands like a hog.

Although I spent countless happy hours playing with all of my Barbie® dolls I do have a few traumatic memories with my Barbie® dolls, too. I remember one particular day when my little brother Seth walked into my room without knocking. I commanded him to get out but he ignored my order. He walked over to the immaculate Barbie® houses, one of which I had painstakingly set the table and positioning all those teeny-tiny little pieces of silverware perfectly was no easy task! I could tell by the look in his eyes that the wheels in his head were spinning wildly. He had a terrible smile of glee on his face and I knew that he was plotting something hideous. I may have been almost four years older than he was but the look on his face left me nearly paralyzed with the fear that disaster was about to befall me. He said, "I want to play Barbies®, too." To my horror I realized that his destructive plan included my favorite toys.

With all the courage I could muster I said, "No! Get out!" But I knew that I was protesting in vain.

The awful smile never left his face. He called out in a mournful, pathetic-sounding tone of voice, "Mommy, Jadie won't share her toys!"

"Jadie, share your toys with your brother," Mom answered. I was doomed and Seth and I both knew it.

Seth still was smiling away. "Let me see Barbie®," he said in a false tone of sweetness.

With no options, I reluctantly handed over my treasured doll. He carefully placed her in the pink elevator that was completely opened on the right hand side. Seth was being so careful I was beginning to think that perhaps he wasn't going to harm her after all. He then began to slowly pull the string and gently took the elevator up three stories to the top. I glanced over at Seth and realized he had pulled the elevator so high up in the air that he was nearly boring a hole in my carpet with the tan plastic pull that made the elevator go up and down. He shot me a look – a maniacal smile. He wanted to make sure that I was paying attention to him. He suddenly let go of the pull string and my Barbie® doll went plummeting down three stories at about eighty miles an hour! When the elevator crashed at the bottom floor, the severe impact threw my poor Barbie® doll out the side and she sailed through the air before crashing into her kitchen table, which collapsed under her weight and knocked down her pink microwave oven, cart and all! The plastic food, little plates and teeny tiny pieces of silverware scattered in all directions. I was dismayed at the destruction that had befallen my poor doll, but that girl was a trooper. Through all of the oppression she never even blinked. She just kept on smiling in happy plastic oblivion. Maybe that's why my brother hated her.

Seth still wasn't satisfied. "Now let me see Ken," he said with the same smile and steady tone of voice that was on the verge of hysterical glee. I was hoping that Ken was as tough as my Barbie® doll, but he was no match for Seth. My brother cheerfully pinched Ken's head between his finger and thumb, flattening Ken's head in the process. Ken never shed a tear; he smiled in the face of his opponent. Seth suddenly wrenched Ken's body and decapitated him. To this day I can still hear the horribly crisp *POP*. Seth was clearly exhilarated by this and grinned ear to ear as he held Ken's body in one hand and Ken's severed head in the other. Seth was making very deliberate eye-contact with me before dropping Ken's body and Ken's head on my nylon carpet. Seth smiled, turned, and walked out the door without a word. He had accomplished his mission that was so mercilessly cruel it only could have been formulated in the mind of a little brother.

I tearfully gathered Ken's remains and carried them to Mommy who was able to re-attach Ken's decapitated head. She would eventually do this many times. I would then go back to my room and excavate my Barbie® doll from the rubble and debris and set about the time consuming task of restoring the Barbie® house to its pre-Seth state.

Even amidst the above mentioned trauma, I did love to play with Barbie® dolls. I eventually owned over thirty dolls as well as a pink Barbie® convertible that had headlights that flipped up from the hood and really lit up. The best part was that it came with a giant pink remote control, which had a black wire about six feet long that attached to the car's rear bumper. By childhood standards any toy that requires four D batteries is one serious toy. I used to love to dress up Barbie® and Ken in their blue jeans, coolest t-shirts, jean jackets, and sunglasses and take them cruising across the linoleum floor of the kitchen or the wooden floor of the enclosed back porch. My Barbie® doll's cool denim outfit was handmade by Grammy Heasley and I had decorated it with wild patterns in silver and glittery red puffy paint.

I wonder just how many hours of my childhood were spent sorting through little Barbie® shoes and rearranging pieces of pink plastic furniture. One thing is for sure, Barbie® dolls were a big part of my childhood and I still have every single Barbie® toy carefully packed away for the day when I have little girls of my own.

Going High-Tech in 1985 with a Home Computer System

I remember visiting my Gram's house as a small child and being in complete awe at a mysterious object belonging to my Uncle Shawn known as an Atari. Its sleek wood grain panels and black grooved top were the epitome of classy design for early 1980s high technology. The gaming system had two joy sticks that plugged into the back of it, and even had a metal switch on it that would allow you to choose whether you wanted to play the game with the graphics in color or in black and white, depending on your television. I would watch in amazement as Shawn played *Pac-Man* and other games, and I was longing to try it. But anytime I got within two or three feet of the Atari Shawn would immediately tell me not to touch it. Looking back, I can't blame him. I was only three or four years old and now I can understand his worries that I might break the video game system if I were to play with it. But in my little youthful mind he didn't have a legitimate concern, he was just being mean. Shawn was my Mom's youngest brother, and he was only nine years older than me. In a lot ways for many years he seemed more like a bratty big brother than an uncle.

One day when my Mom and I were visiting my Gram, Shawn wasn't home. I looked at the forbidden video game console and felt the need to take some sort of revenge against it. I was armed with a box of Cracker Jacks that Mom had bought for me. I asked Mom to open the box and went out to the living room where the prominently displayed Atari held a place of honor. In those days I would eat all the popcorn out of the Cracker Jacks first and save the peanuts for last. Why I chose to eat Cracker Jacks systematically is a mystery that defies explanation, even by me. I sat down right in front of his Atari and decided to use it as a plate. I savored my well-plotted rebellion (give me a break, I was only three or four) more than I savored my snack. As I found each peanut I carefully placed it on the Atari and ate all the popcorn out of the box and then ate every peanut off the Atari one by one. I was impressed when I finished my snack and looked at the Atari and it was still in perfect shape. If I could eat sticky snack food off of the Atari and have it still be in good working order shouldn't that be proof that I could play games on the Atari without hurting it?

I remember once after that day I asked Shawn's permission to play the Atari. He said "No!" in such a harsh tone that I was thinking he was probably showing off for the friend he had invited over more than he was answering my question.

Anger boiled in me as I shot back in a preschooler's rage, "Oh yeah? I ate a whole bunch of Cracker Jacks off your Atari one time when you weren't here!" He glared at me with such fury that I ran out the front door and into the yard hoping that he would be too lazy to tattle on me. I still remember the fear I felt as I tightly clutched my little Strawberry Shortcake doll in one hand and my Apricot doll in the other that I had been carrying around. I knew if he told on me I would get in trouble, even though Shawn had it coming. Even worse I knew that Mommy would make me apologize to Shawn which would be a fatal blow to my pride, after all he did deserve the Cracker Jack revenge. My plot to avoid punishment was simple: Sit on the porch and play with Strawberry Shortcake and Apricot and make it look like someone as sweet and cute and innocent as me wasn't capable of hatching and executing such a nefarious plot. I was only out there a few minutes, the smell of fear mingling with the heavy artificial fragrance of strawberry and apricot that the vinyl dolls perpetually emanated. Since Mom never came out to ask me about my plan of Atari sabotage I figured Shawn hadn't bothered to tattle on me so I slipped back into the house quietly and was on my best behavior for the rest of the visit.

There was another particular time that Shawn wasn't home so I decided to switch tactics. I timidly asked my Gram, "Can I play Shawn's Atari?"

Gram looked at me and must have realized that visions of *Pac-Man* were dancing in my head because she said, "Go ahead, Jadie." I was thrilled! My Mom helped me set the Atari up and I was overjoyed at the electronic privilege to fearlessly lead Pac-Man through the blinking maze, eating pellets and dodging ghosts.

In 1985 my Dad, a mechanic by trade, worked for small company that sold computers and computer equipment. One winter day Mom decided to let me in on a secret and said, "Tomorrow Daddy is bringing home an Atari!" An Atari! I couldn't have been more excited if she said Daddy was the new Vice President and we were all going to move to the White House so our whole family could help President Reagan run the country.

"Are we getting an Atari just like Shawn's?" I practically squealed with excitement.

"No," Mom smiled, "it's bigger and better than Shawn's!"

Bigger and better than Shawn's! My joy knew no bounds! I spent the next day trying to keep busy by playing with my toys but the word, "Atari" wouldn't leave my mind and the day seemed to drag on for eternity. Finally after it was dark outside Daddy came home and marched through the front door with a huge white cardboard box. It was like he had pulled a treasure chest from the bottom of the sea. He set it down and went right back outside. I asked my Mom where he was going and she said he had to go and get the rest of the computer. *The rest of the computer? There's more?*

By the time Dad had finished carrying in all the parts and pieces of the computer and hooked them up I was amazed. The main Atari console looked like a huge brown plastic typewriter and the top popped open to reveal the hidden compartment where metal game cartridges were inserted. There was a massive floppy disk drive, two huge joy sticks, a dot matrix printer (which was a new concept to me entirely), and a small metal box that attached to the back of the TV to transform a mere television into a computer screen. I was in complete awe. Daddy also brought home two games: *Cocoa Notes*, and *Peanut Butter Panic*.

I remember that night and the next day Mom and I sat down in front of the TV and played the awesome video games. I couldn't believe how real the pictures looked! Mom was right, this was better than Shawn's Atari. I remember a few days later when Daddy put a great big *Print Shop* floppy disk in the disk drive and showed me that we now had the power to make our own greeting cards, signs, and even five-foot long banners! I sat on his lap and designed a greeting card. He flipped through all of the available pictures one at a time so I could choose one, then he let me pick out the font, the design of the border, and decide whether the card would be printed in black ink (which in reality was more dark gray than black), or colored stripes. I watched in amazement as the printer hummed and buzzed and pulled the tractor-feed paper in, and finally the printer head screeched its way across the paper to print the first line. After about ten minutes the printer head pulled back and screeched out the second line. I couldn't believe the power that the Atari had given me. About six days later, the printer had completed the greeting card. All we had to do was remove the perforated strips from the sides of the paper and fold the card into quarters.

I vividly recall the first time Mom used the printer. She was waiting for some project to print, but was concerned that the printer was broken because it printed the first line, but seemingly did nothing after that. I assured her that it was okay, it just took a long time for things to print. She wasn't certain that I had grown so computer savvy in less than a week. Eventually the printer did finish the job and Mom was impressed that I had acquired so much knowledge of this new technological marvel in such a short period of time. But that was the beautiful fact about computers in the early 1980s: they were so simple a child could use them.

Now it seems funny to me that people in my Mom's extended family came over for the sole purpose of seeing the computer similar to the way they had when Mom had brought my newborn baby brother home from the hospital a few months earlier. I remember they were astounded by the Atari 800 Home Computer System. One person marveled, "Do you mean that's a typewriter that you hook up to the television? You don't even have to put paper in it?" Everyone was impressed by it. At that time we were the only family out of everyone we knew that owned a home computer.

Ironically, with all the fears that Shawn had that I would hurt his Atari, he was the one that ended up messing up ours about a year later (well, sort of). By this time our selection of video games had expanded and he came over to play a game one night. I would have been much happier if I would have been allowed to tell him that he couldn't play our Atari since I couldn't play his, but I knew that Mom would never let me say anything like that.

Shawn popped a floppy disk into the big grayish-white plastic disk drive and the television began making a series of beeping noises that were completely foreign to me. The words, "BOOT ERROR" appeared at the top of the screen and suddenly the words had made a long list down the screen of "BOOT ERROR BOOT ERROR BOOT ERROR BOOT ERROR BOOT ERROR." "What's 'boot error' mean?" he asked Mom in a worried tone.

"Oh, it's nothing, just pop the disk out and put it back in," Mom answered. He did, and the Atari worked fine. I was relieved that the Atari was okay, but was disappointed that Shawn didn't get into any trouble for making the computer do something that it wasn't supposed to.

Many years later I would get on another computer and access something new called "the internet." I found a website devoted to Atari history and I was surprised to learn that Atari had ceased production of the Atari 800 in 1982. Our computer was brand new when we got it in 1985, so I guess that the computer sales company my Dad worked for must have had some left over. At that time home computer systems were so rare that it didn't seem to matter that it was a model that was no longer being produced, it was still really advanced for that time.

Over the years we amassed quite the collection of Atari games. Some of my favorites included: *Pac-Man, Donkey Kong, Summer Games, Pole Position, Pitfall, Zork II* (which took me about three years to figure out how to play), *Asteroids, Frogger, Cocoa Notes, Peanut Butter Panic,* and *River Raid.* Seth even had the infamous *E.T. the Extra-Terrestrial* game, which I never figured out at all or got past the first level. But apparently I wasn't the only one. To this day that cartridge is buried in the attic, and if the internet rumors are true, Atari buried about five million E.T. game cartridges along with seven million Pac-Man cartridges that were either unsold or returned. Supposedly the cartridges were steamrolled, buried in a pit in either an Arizona or New Mexico landfill, and cemented over to prevent looting.

Although I never owned Q-Bert myself, one of my cousins did and I always enjoyed playing that game. It's only fitting and proper that Q-Bert be mentioned in any list of classic 1980s video games.

33

I have to say that the Atari was probably my most favorite purchase my parents ever made, even including our house and my college education.

The VCR: The Must Have High Technology Status Symbol

Around the time that my parents bought the Atari they also bought a VCR. Although I don't remember all the big exciting moments leading up to getting the VCR the way I remember the Atari, I was still very impressed with the VCR. Up until the time when Daddy brought it home and hooked the big silvery metal box to the TV I had no clue that such wondrous devices even existed. Daddy was the captain of a mighty ship sailing on the high seas of high technology with the $375, two head Video Cassette Recorder. It looked really impressive hooked up to our color television that had three knobs and no remote control, but for those times it was a perfectly nice and respectable TV. I remember that we had three tapes – two of which I can't remember what they were because I wasn't allowed to watch them. I'm guessing they were probably rated PG and my parents weren't anxious for me to see any movies where the main characters weren't wholesome cartoon characters or puppets, but I can't blame them since I was so little. However, Daddy did pick out one special tape for me, *The Muppets Take Manhattan*. I loved that movie and the concept that I could control what the TV had on it was mind-boggling. Not only could I watch the movie whenever I wanted, I could watch whatever individual part of the movie that I wanted. My favorite moments of that movie were when the rats sang that scatting, jazzy song and cooked breakfast, and when Miss Piggy had a flashback to her childhood that introduced the Muppet Babies to the world. Apparently I wasn't the only one impressed, because according to what I read later on this scene got such a high response that it resulted in the Emmy-award winning *Muppet Babies* cartoon, which became a critical part of my Saturday morning routine for years to come. Although I was always sad to see the show come to an end, the pain was soothed by watching Animal commit one final act of mischief (usually at the expense of Gonzo) and then happily yelling, "Go bye bye!" When I was old enough to go to school Mom gave me my choice of any lunch box in Gee Bee's, and I picked out a metal Muppet Babies lunch box for $2.99 that I still steadfastly believe was the coolest lunch box in all of human history. I remember the price because it took me forever to pick the sticky paper price tag off it, which Mom was able to remove the rest of when she washed it before she packed me a lunch in it for the first time. Those lunches usually consisted of a sandwich, a pack of Tastykakes, and a 25¢ bag of Middleswarth Sour Cream and Onion Chips, and the included yellow Baby Kermit thermos was filled with milk. If you live away from the Northeastern seaboard and have never had a Tastykake or Middleswarth Chips you have my deepest sympathies.

The stupendous VCR transformed what was once an ordinary living room with a color television into our own personal movie theatre. I was astounded to learn that not only could we watch pre-recorded movies; we could buy blank tapes and record movies and shows off the television! I remember when we were recording *The*

Wizard of Oz during its yearly broadcast that I very quietly whispered a question into Mommy's ear concerning the scary green floating head of the Wizard, which I found mildly disturbing. I wanted to know what Judy Garland was actually talking to. I was relieved that she was merely having a conversation with a film strip. I then told Mommy that I didn't want to talk loudly because I didn't want the VCR to record what I said because it would be stuck in the movie. I was very impressed to learn that the VCR was brilliant enough to record the sounds and words from the television without recording the words and sounds from the room. Was there no end to this marvelous machine's capabilities?

For all of the Americans who owned VCRs during this time this new technological wonder meant two things: one, it was a status symbol and if you had a VCR you were hot stuff. Secondly, it meant that you were now free to make plans outside of the house whenever you wanted and never had to miss anything on the television. You could merely program the metal genius to tape whatever it was you wanted to see. What was really impressive was the luxury of being able to fast forward through the commercials. Another extraordinary factor was that you could tape a program but watch something else on another channel. It was a grand day in the Heasley house when we realized that if we were taping a movie one of us could hit the "stop" button and cut out all the commercials, and when the commercial break was over somebody could hit "record" and we would have a nearly seamless film with no interruptions.

I remember my Mom telling me that some women bought VCRs for the sole purpose of taping shows and pausing close-ups of certain stars to see exactly how they did their make-up. Although why these women weren't smart enough to just go spend two dollars on a fashion magazine instead of spending three or four hundred dollars on a VCR is beyond me.

Just like with the computer, my parents were the only people we knew that had a VCR for quite some time. I remember when I went to elementary school and the few of us whose parents had VCRs would talk about the movies we had on VCR tapes. The mere mention of the letters "VCR" brought looks of awe and wonder from the other children. I remember in the first grade all the teachers cleared their class schedules so that the entire first grade could watch a movie on a VCR. About sixty to seventy kids sat like little Indians (that expression was not politically incorrect at that time) on the carpeted floor of one of the classrooms that had all the desks moved to the sides of the room. We all stared intently at the eighteen inch television that sat on top of a metal cart. When the movie was interrupted by a commercial break another child and I told the teacher that we could skip the commercials if she pressed the fast forward button. She had yet to hear of this concept and seemed impressed by our brilliance.

It seems funny now that all of us little first graders sat down in that crowded classroom and were completely excited to watch a movie on a VCR. Sure, it was fun to get out of class and see a movie, but half of the fun was the fact that we were watching it on a VCR. We sat there with our little smiles, most of us missing at least one front baby tooth with a partially showing grown-up tooth trying to take its place, waiting for the movie to begin. It seems funny that we were so anxious to see a movie from a VHS cassette tape because in a lot of ways watching a filmstrip from a projector would have been far more practical because the screen would have been six times larger. But for as much as we were impressed by the VCR, we would be absolutely stunned the following year when the school bought two Apple computers for every classroom. Up until that point I had never seen a computer monitor before, at least not in person. I grew to treasure the opportunities I had to use the computer because *Number Munchers* was a fun game, but the ultimate educational video game was *Oregon Trail*. I remember trying to buy things at the trading post to trade to other pioneers later on, attempting to cross rivers without having my wagon go under, and shooting buffalo and any other little critters that happened to flicker across the screen. That was a great game.

I remember when my Mom video-taped the movie *Short Circuit*. She was pretty strict about what my brother and I were allowed to watch so when an edited movie aired on television we were always happy to add another cool movie to the collection. I thought that Number Five was the greatest robot ever, even better than C3PO, R2-D2 and Rosie from *The Jetsons*. I was impressed when Number Five appeared as a special guest on the Nickelodeon TV show *Don't Just Sit There*. That movie gave me the dream of wanting to build a robot. I tried to build one out of regular Lego bricks but it wasn't the same thing as a real robot that was made of metal and could talk and move on its own. I've yet to achieve this feat.

Over the years VCRs came down in price and as more and more people owned them a whole new type of business sprang up: video rental stores. No matter how tiny your town was you probably had at least one video rental store, as well as two or three grocery and convenience stores that rented video tapes. The town I grew up in was small, and I believe by 1988 the town had four hundred times the amount of rental tapes than it did citizens. Even the town library began to stock educational tapes that could be borrowed overnight. Typically a few times a month Mom would walk my brother and I down town to the video store to pick out two and sometimes even three movies. Usually she picked out one for her and Dad to watch, and Seth and I alternated turns choosing a kid-friendly movie. But sometimes if both of us behaved really well we each got to choose a movie. This was really generous of her since it cost Mom eight or nine dollars to rent three movies for two nights, which at that time could buy almost a full tank of gas for our family car, Bessie the Station Wagon.

But time marches on and eventually the DVD player began to phase out VCRs. Even though VCRs and VCR tapes are now considered ancient artifacts no one can deny that they were once valuable and essential items for showing off your financial status in the 1980s.

Now early VCR tapes are really beginning to show themselves valuable in a whole new way: as time capsules. Movies and shows with the commercial breaks included are now more fun to watch than the program itself. The older the commercial the more entertaining it happens to be. You can always tell how old a VCR tape is by how heavy it is. If it is lighter weight the tape is newer. If it weighs more than a pound because it has metal parts in it, you know you have a truly vintage tape in your hands.

An Orange Squirt Gun and Angry Neighbors

The Super Soaker water gun first appeared in 1989, which means that the majority of water battles were far more tame than they would be after the spectacular Super Soaker's grand debut. I remember when I was about five-years-old Aunt Kelly bought me a bright orange squirt gun. It was a basic, simple squirt gun and I didn't think that it shot very far, probably only a few feet, but it was my first squirt gun and I thought it was awesome. I was outside on a nice spring day, and it must have been a Saturday since Daddy was home, it wasn't a Sunday morning or we would have been in church. I was happily running around the backyard and randomly squirting water at invisible targets because my brother would have only been about a year old and he wasn't old enough to be in a squirt gun battle. I wish Mom would have let him play water battle with me, he wouldn't have been armed because he was barely out of his baby days and that would have made him an easy target in what would ultimately be an undeniable victory.

Nonetheless I was running through the yard that was fenced-in and stranger proof squirting imaginary adversaries in the eye when one of the neighbors had a guest leaving their home, which was also a beauty shop. He was a man with white hair and a big white beard and the fact that he was rather rotund caught my attention. I decided to pretend to squirt him. He seemed to be about twenty or twenty-five feet away so I knew that my little squirt gun would never reach him, so what was the harm? I can still remember the pale blue, short-sleeved dress shirt he was wearing as he proudly came down the two or three cement stairs from the side door of the beauty shop sporting a new hair cut. I took aim and began to rapidly and repeatedly squeeze the trigger of the squirt gun and he started to yell at me. What was he being such a big baby about? Despite his protesting I kept on squirting. It wasn't like the water could go that far from that little tiny toy that I was holding in my little tiny hands. But then I noticed a curious thing. His pale blue shirt now had a dark blue spot on it that was about four or five inches across. *Wow!* I thought to myself. I had no idea that the little squirt gun had such a long range. I was pleased that the small orange squirt gun had exceeded my expectations, but celebrating would have to be postponed because the screaming and scowling meant that it was time to flee. The rationale running through my little head was that if I run, I would be leaving them alone and they would be happy. Maybe they would just be thankful that I wasn't being pesky. Besides, if I was in my house on my best behavior Mommy and Daddy and would surely doubt the neighbor lady's ludicrous claim that I was launching aquatic attacks from our backyard.

I darted in the house, left the water gun on the enclosed back porch, and as casually as I could I strolled into the kitchen where Mommy and Daddy were talking. I sat in my chair with perfect posture just like a perfect little lady who would most certainly not be wreaking watery havoc on the neighborhood. Mommy looked over at me and said, "What have you been up to, sweetie?"

"Oh, nothing, just playing in the backyard," I said in the most innocent tone of voice that I could muster.

"Having fun?" Daddy asked.

I shrugged. "Yeah, I guess." I couldn't make it look like I had really been up to something. Mommy and Daddy continued to talk about boring grownup stuff. Everything in the kitchen was so peaceful and serene I thought I had escaped from the awkward situation of saturating the Scary Man's shirt. But then the neighbor lady decided to tell Mommy and Daddy what had happened. Suddenly my well thought out plan had taken an unexpected turn. Why did grownups have to go and tattletale on poor defenseless little girls?

"Did you squirt someone who was leaving the beauty shop?" Mommy asked.

"Um, no, not really," I said as innocently as I could. I wasn't lying according to the little system of logic that I had quickly devised. I didn't know the water gun could shoot so far and therefore I didn't squirt him on purpose. That was far different than actually intentionally squirting someone, or so I thought.

Mommy looked at me and asked, "Is the neighbor lady lying to Daddy and I?"

Good theory! Fantastic thought! I liked that idea and I wanted to run with it. The only problem was that Mommy was using her "loud question" tone of voice which meant that she already knew the answer.

Experience had taught me that her loud question tone came shortly before I got punished.

"Um, maybe not," I said.

Daddy was beginning to get that stern look on his face that I knew quite well and said, "If you didn't squirt him and she's not lying something isn't right. You better tell me the truth right now or you're in big trouble, young lady."

Hmm. Another unexpected twist. They asked me for an explanation point blank. So I told them the whole truth. "Well, I pointed the squirt gun at him and I pulled the trigger but I was standing really, really, really far away and I didn't think he was going to get wet," I said.

"Well, he did," Mommy said. "You can go next door and apologize."

Apologize to the Scary Man who yelled!? She's got to be kidding! Did Mommy have the slightest idea of the doom and the wrath that surely awaited me? Judging by how bent out of shape the Scary Man got I figured that he probably made little kids work as slaves before he cooked them and ate them for lunch! His house was probably made out of gingerbread to boot!

"Where is your squirt gun?" Daddy asked.

"On the porch," I answered.

"Go get it," he said.

Reluctantly, I got up from the chair and brought my cool new toy to Daddy. He pulled the little clear plug from the back of the squirt gun and began to empty what was left of the water down the drain. Then he did something horrible and unthinkable. He put my wonderful little orange squirt gun on top of the refrigerator! The refrigerator was taller than Mommy! It was almost as tall as Daddy! He may as well have put it on top of a sky scraper! Now what? What was going to happen to my poor little orange squirt gun? Daddy said, "You can have your squirt gun back when you prove you can be responsible with it." I stood there and felt my heart sink, as though it were being washed away down the drain like the water that had been inside the squirt gun. How was I supposed to be responsible? I was just a little kid. What did I have to do be responsible? Buy a house? Drive a car? Get a job? Vote in the next election? I was too little to vote. I couldn't vote until I was a grown up. I was also too little to get a job or drive a car or buy a house. It was beginning to look like I wouldn't see my lovely little squirt gun again until the end of time.

Mommy and Daddy made me go and apologize to the neighbor lady, which I did as nicely as I could although none of the grownups seemed to get the fact that I didn't think that the water would actually reach the Scary Man. But I was happy to know that my little orange squirt gun had proven itself to be one of outstanding quality. One thing that disappointed me was that even though I went next door and apologized right away (thankfully the Scary Man was gone by this point or I might not have lived to see the sun set that day), the neighbor lady seemed cranky about the whole thing. Why? She was usually nice to me. I said I was sorry. I just didn't get what her obvious attitude problem was about.

I would eventually get my squirt gun back. It was probably a few weeks until we were reunited. Mommy told me that I wasn't allowed to squirt anyone unless they also had a water gun and it was a water battle she approved of. I listened, too, at least until I was a teenager. The first of two joys that I would discover later on was that if I was riding in a bus and had the window open and I sprayed a mini squirt gun out the window at a forty five degree angle the force of the wind around the moving bus would catapult the water into the faces of the people behind me. This was fun because it took them a minute or two to figure out where the water was coming from. Since they didn't say anything to me, how was I supposed to know that the water was hitting them, or that they minded the refreshing experience that I was providing them on that hot day in early summer? Now I never would have tried this on public or school transportation due to the massive amount of trouble I could have gotten into; I made this particular water prank discovery on a church bus. Since I stopped shooting water when they told me to the kind people sitting behind me quickly forgave and forgot my teenage transgression. I was too young and naive to realize that I could have caused someone to have a problem with their contact lenses if the water had hit them in the eye.

The second joyful prank I learned was that if I took a small squirt gun and shot it straight out of a window (a screened window worked) from two stories up when a person was walking underneath it, especially if there were lots of trees nearby, the water would hit the person and make them think that some vicious bird had splattered a vile souvenir on their head. It was always so much fun to see the prank victim's shocked, horrified, and livild expression as their eyes angrily darted back and forth from tree to tree trying to find the bold bird that had dared to defecate in their hair. Oh, the joys of youth!

But as I look back on the events of that morning in my early childhood I have only one regret: No one took a picture of the Scary Man's shirt. The big dark blue spot on his light blue shirt wasn't that far from the very center of his chest, which was where I was aiming. I really did have remarkable marksmanship.

Christmas Cheer and Christmas Fear

Who can ever forget the childhood anticipation of Christmas? For me the Christmas season began to creep in during the month of September when Sears sent out their annual Christmas Wishbook. Every year I was elated when the mailman brought the thick catalogue and I would eagerly skip past all the boring pages of clothing and bed spreads and flip to the section that contained the most jubilant consumer product in the history of the world: Toys. The toy section was a superb source of joy. It splashed color and excitement at me in the form of thousands of pictures of all the toys that were available to me in this one incredible book. There were Barbie® dolls and accessories, Tasty Bake Ovens, Craft Kits, Magic Kits, Detective Kits, Makit Bakit Ovens, games, and countless forms of incredible toys. I would eagerly study page after page, and then compile a gargantuan Christmas list that would be added to throughout the year as the toy commercials grew more plentiful and abundant as Christmas came closer.

Very early in my childhood my parents began a tradition that would officially kickoff the holiday season at our house. On Thanksgiving morning they would give my brother and I two or three Christmas ornaments each, always gift wrapped in white tissue paper. For Seth and I this was a lot of fun and we eagerly waited for Thanksgiving morning. We greedily shredded apart the tissue paper to see what new ornaments would be added to our collection. Dad would always go up to the attic and get our boxes of ornaments from previous years and Seth and I would go through our individual collections. Mom had begun a list on the inside of each of our box lids of ornaments, keeping a chronological list of each ornament, who had given it to us, and what year we had received it. By the time Seth and I reached adulthood we each had over one hundred ornaments.

We always watched the Macy's Thanksgiving Day Parade while going through our ornament collection, which had also become a tradition in our house. It took Mom quite a few years of convincing and reminding me that the parade was officially called, "The Macy's Thanksgiving Day Parade," not "The Macy's Day Parade." I loved to watch the parade progress through Times Square and seemingly right into our living room. It was especially exciting when the wind was really strong and the gust caused the balloon handlers to scramble and try to keep the balloon under control. I paid close attention to these moments to see if the balloon would sweep the balloon handlers off their feet. What would it be like to march in the parade as a balloon handler? Would it be anything like ringing the massive cast iron bell at our church? Every Sunday morning between Sunday School and the Worship Service a grownup man would start to ring the church bell, while a group of three or four kids waited to take over the job once the bell was ringing. It required a lot of muscle power to keep the bell going, a group of three or four kids would pull as hard as they could on the thick, antiquated rope that ran what seemed to be one hundred feet into the air and into a small hole in the ceiling that would tilt the massive cast iron bell in the steeple. No sooner would we have pulled the rope down a foot or two the weight of the bell would instantly snap the rope back up again in what was more or less a challenging game of tug-o-war. I remember being about five or six-years-old and a group of us were ringing the bell and I remember feeling like the rope was going to pick me up in the air, and I was kind of wishing that it would. I used to love to ring that bell and hear its ancient clang echo throughout the sanctuary.

December the 1st brought another seasonal gift from Mom: advent calendars. They were little cardboard calendars with cardboard doors that were perforated so that we could pop one open each day of the month until Christmas Eve. Sometimes Mom would get each of us our own calendar, and sometimes she would get us one that was really big and fancy for us to share. One year Seth and I each got a calendar that was a big 3-D Victorian village. It was folded like a fan, each fold had a different shop printed on it and the best part was that the calendar was scratch and sniff. There were pine scents, cinnamon, and bread, among others. It was really neat.

A few years later Mom bought us an advent calendar to share that was really elaborate. It was a big pop-up, multi-layered paperboard orchestra of angels. It even had a string and when you pulled it some of the angels would draw their bows back and forth over their violins and the others would move their hands back and forth across their harps.

As all goodhearted people know, Christmas isn't just about receiving. The spirit of giving was instilled in me by Mom. When you're a child gift giving is the best and most enjoyable giving you will ever experience in your life because you don't have to spend your own money. I remember one year my elementary school set up Santa's Secret Workshop. This consisted of tables of small gift items that would range in price from one dollar to a few dollars. Mom would give me money to pick out presents for her, Dad, and Seth. One year I bought Seth a big, two tone glow-in-the-dark super ball. This was during an era when glow-in-the-dark toys were really awesome and considered a big deal. I meticulously wrapped up the super ball and put it under the tree with the other presents that had arrived from Grandma Annette and our step-grandfather, Grandpa Aronne. Seth looked at the wrapped present I had carefully selected for him and said, "You got me a super ball."

"Not uh," I said. I don't know why I thought I could fool him; I guess I just wanted it to be a surprise.

Seth took the super ball, still in its wrapping paper, and dropped it on the exposed wooden floor that separated the double living room. When he dropped the super ball it hit the floor with a quick thud and then bounced wildly. "Yeah it is. See?" he proclaimed with a sore winner's sneer.

I responded by glaring at him as hard as I could and then tattled on him for snooping. I took all of my big sister duties very seriously, and as any older sister will tell you dirty looks and tattling are two of the most important responsibilities of having a younger sibling.

After the age of Mom giving me money for Santa's Secret Work Shop I took great pride in spending my own money on presents. Every child in the 1980s knew that there was one splendid store that allowed you to buy pretty much anything for anyone for almost no money at all: The Dollar Store! One of the most beautiful aspects of buying gifts with your own money is that grownups think whatever you give them is grand because you spent your own money and picked out a gift for them all by yourself. Of course you have the rest of your life to buy gifts for your family that you will pick out yourself and pay for with your own money. Sadly, the privilege of buying one item for them from a dollar store expires when you're about eleven. But once the gifts were purchased for my family it was time to focus on the stash that St. Nicholas would be leaving under the tree for me.

Mom would always take us to see Santa on multiple occasions. We would see him downtown in the little Santa's Workshop that sat next to the Fire Station, we would see him at the mall, at Hill's Department Store, he'd visit the elementary school, he'd come to my Dad's company Christmas party, and we would see him again at Candy Cane Lane in South Williamsport, a street where every house tried to have the most elaborate display of lights and Christmas decorations. Santa would be casually strolling up and down the street, stopping at every car to give a candy cane to each child. Candy Cane Lane and Dad's company Christmas party were the only times we would ever see Santa Claus at night. Mom would always take us to see Santa during the day, but she would go and see Santa in the evenings. She told us that Santa would stay late at the store because he always wanted to talk to the parents when kids weren't along so the parents could tell Santa how their kids were really behaving. It always took her a few hours because she had to stand in a long line with all the other parents who were waiting to talk to Santa. Mom would also be sure to fill him in on the things that we wanted, just to make sure that he remembered everything. She would also take lots of money with her to pay Santa to bring us the toys we wanted. Besides taking money along, she also left a box of money under the tree on Christmas Eve for Santa to pay for the rest of the toys that he had acquired after Mom's final visit to the store. Seth and I left him milk and cookies on the dining room table, but Mom never put out the money box out until after we went to bed. She said that it wouldn't be polite for Seth and I to see how much money there was.

On Christmas Eve my Mom's entire extended family would get together at Gram's house for a wonderful Christmas feast of baked ham, browned potatoes, and about thirty-five other fantastic side dishes. As good as the dinner was my favorite part was always dessert. Gram Harman made the most amazing iced sugar cookies that were so soft that if you dunked them in milk they would fall apart. Gram also made peanut blossom cookies with a Hershey's Kiss in the center. Those cookies were incredibly good. Gram also kept dishes of candy on the mantle, Brach's mint nougats with green Christmas trees in the center, and candy straws with chocolate cream centers. She also welcomed everyone to help themselves to the brightly colored, cherry flavored candy canes that hung on the tree. She also had a string of antique Christmas lights with the gigantic colored glass bulbs on the tree. I remember her gently cautioning me when I was very young, "Jadie, you can get a candy cane from the tree but please be really careful not to touch the lights. Those old lights get really hot and they will burn your skin if you touch one." I heeded her words and always picked the candy canes that were furthest from the blazing hot bulbs. I never did get burned.

After dinner most of us would go to the Christmas Eve service at the church we attended. Seth and I usually had a part in the Christmas Eve Nativity with the other children. It was at these moments that it really felt like Christmas with candles glowing and hearing all about how God sent His Son little Baby Jesus to save the world. Once the play was over I used to love to go back to the old wooden pew and sit with my family and sing those wonderful old Christmas hymns that were written more than one hundred years earlier. The blasting pipe organ nearly shook the old plaster walls of the church as the organist played each hymn. The organ also controlled the big set of chimes that hung on the back wall of the church, which sounded beautiful. As a child I marveled at the mystery of how the chimes were played from the organ that sat one hundred feet away. We heard a Christmas message from our pastor, Lynn, whom I greatly admired.

Our church was close to our house, probably less than a quarter of a mile. I remember sitting in the back seat of the station wagon on the way home from the service thinking that Daddy was driving too slowly. I had to get home and get into bed as soon as possible so that Santa Claus would have plenty of time to come to our house and leave all my presents. Christmas Eve was the only night of the year I went to bed voluntarily. After I went to bed Santa Claus would come and fill the stockings that Mom made for Seth and I with toys and candy, and he would leave each of us a massive pile of gifts. One year a friend of the family had stockings made for Seth and I, and so after that Mom allowed us each to hang two stockings and Santa always filled both of them. Mom later confessed that she was worried if we had to choose one stocking, we wouldn't pick the one she made because it was smaller than the one's given to us by the friend of the family. When people came over to visit at Christmas time and saw that Seth and I each had two stockings they would immediately ask why. Instead of filling them in on the whole scoop I would simply answer, "One for each foot." I have to say that I have always enjoyed people's confused looks over my twisted sense of logic. I especially enjoyed getting double the amount of stocking stuffers, such as lip balm (which wasn't quite as fun as real lipstick, but it was close enough), candy, small toys, and film for my 110 camera.

I always had an incredibly hard time falling asleep on Christmas Eve, mostly because I was so excited and partly because I have naturally been a night owl my entire life. One Christmas Eve when I was five or six I fell asleep but woke up when it was still dark outside. I knew that the morning officially started before the sun came up so as quietly as I could I crept through the hallway in the pitch black, past Seth's bedroom where he was sound asleep, to ask Mommy and Daddy if it was okay to get up. I snuck into their room and gently shook Mommy's shoulder. "Can we get up yet?" I asked.

"What time is it?" she asked sleepily, while looking over at her and Daddy's alarm clock with the glowing red digital numbers. "It's only midnight, morning is several hours away. Santa probably hasn't even come yet."

Suddenly a noise in the distance caught my attention. I heard the sound of a gently ringing bell. I stood still in complete silence thinking ecstatically, *It's Santa!*

Mom must have heard it too because she whispered, "Jadie, do you think that might be-?"

"Yeah!" I whispered. Mom had sewn a bell on the toe of the stocking that she had made me and I was convinced that Santa Claus was downstairs in the living room at that very moment filling my stocking with presents. It never occurred to me until years later that it might have been the bell on Seth's stocking that I heard. But that would have been ridiculous. Why would Santa be filling Seth's stocking when he could have been filling mine?

"You better get back to bed before Santa realizes you're awake!" Mommy whispered.

As quickly and quietly as I could I raced back to bed. I never dared to peek down the stairs to try to see Santa. I couldn't risk blowing my cover and having him take all my presents back to the North Pole.

I remember fantastic gifts, and my most favorite one that Santa ever brought for me was the Barbie® house I got when I was four. When Seth wasn't busy wreaking havoc on Barbie's® house it was the site of many lavish dinner parties. Barbie® and Ken were dressed to the nines and invited Mr. and Mrs. Heart, P.J., and all the dolls that I owned, who were dressed in their best formal wear and I made sure that all the guests had their hair perfectly styled. Barbie® always served a delicious meal of microwaved chicken and plastic pie for desert.

When I was two Santa Claus brought me a Baby Ann doll. I don't remember that particular Christmas, but I loved Baby Ann and probably played with her more than any other doll I had when I was little. She came with a car seat and a little diaper bag that had a bottle, dish, and a baby spoon. He also brought me a homemade Cabbage Patch Doll when I was four that I named Rebecca. She had brown hair and brown eyes just like me. When I was in Kindergarten Santa got me a Chatty Patty doll. She came with a little purse full of accessories such as a mirror, a comb, a puppy, a present, and a few other items. Each piece had a plastic stick attached that fit perfectly into her molded plastic fist. When you pulled her string she talked about whatever item she was holding, which was just about the coolest thing I had ever seen. I used to comb Chatty Patty's nylon hair while she was holding her mirror, and then I'd pull the string so she could admire my stupendous hair styling skills. How did Chatty Patty have such a vast understanding of the world around her like that? A few years later Santa brought me a store bought Cabbage Patch Doll named Kitty Kora, who also had brown hair and brown eyes just like me. She was even wearing a pair of glasses, which was cool for her. Unfortunately I ended up wearing glasses myself before the decade was over, which wasn't cool for me.

I also remember the year that Santa gave me a Show n' Tell Phono Viewer that was a projector and a record player. It came with a slide strip with individual pictures that could be watched on a small screen, or, with the flip of a switch the unit would project a four foot image on the wall! I usually just opted to watch the little screen, because I had floral wall paper and when I set the story to projector mode everything in the picture ended up being tattooed with pink rose buds, which was really annoying. Don't get me wrong, I loved my wallpaper but not plastered across Peter Pan's face. The Show n' Tell Phono Viewer played an included 45rpm record that narrated the story. The record would automatically cause the projector to flip to the next picture as the story unfolded. It was amazing! Santa also brought several other story sets to go with it and it was like having my own personal movie theatre. I loved it.

One year Santa gave me a Play-Doh Mop Top Hair Shop that was a beauty shop with two plastic people with tons of tiny holes in their heads and little beauty shop accessories, including a pair of scissors. The chair of the beauty shop had a crank that would extrude the Play-Doh through their scalps and let them grow an awesome head of Play-Doh hair that could be cut and styled. Sometimes I pretended that the little man was Jon Bon Jovi and I would make his hair really big and wild. But I couldn't cut his hair until after I quit pretending that he was Jon Bon Jovi because trimming Jon's locks would have been unthinkable. I spent many happy hours cutting salty smelling blue hair because of that toy.

I remember that Monopoly was what I wanted most when I was seven, and Santa brought it. I'm hoping that one day I can accumulate great wealth by using the real estate tycoon skills I developed from that game.

Another year Santa brought me a Deluxe Pee-Wee's Playhouse set and every Pee-Wee Herman action figure that I didn't already own. Over the years Santa brought tons of toys and games, sleds, Crayola sets and craft kits. But one thing that Santa insisted on bringing was clothing and it drove me up the wall. Who wants boring old clothes? I sure didn't. Once I opened up the box to confirm that it was an outfit, I set it aside without even taking it out of the box. I just didn't understand it. Of course I liked having cool clothes, but I thought all the money that Mom and Dad gave Santa should be spent on fun things, not stupid necessities. I firmly believed that it was Mom and Dad's responsibility to clothe me, and Santa's job to bring the fun stuff. As a kid I thought that Santa bringing clothes was two steps away from bringing groceries and Children's Tylenol.

All of the gifts that Santa left in our stockings and under the tree were wrapped up in paper, but Seth and I knew that Santa always brought us one thing that wasn't gift wrapped. When we were finished opening presents we went into the dining room where we had left Santa some milk and cookies. We would find the dining room table with an empty glass, the cookie plate bare with the exception of a few crumbs, and next to it would be a brown paper lunch bag. This bag would contain all the batteries we would need for our new toys.

It was Christmas of 1986 when I was ripping the wrapping paper off of my gifts from Santa that I had noticed something that left me somewhat disturbed, but I swallowed my doubts and kept opening presents. Later on after all the gifts were opened I went up to Mom and asked her, somewhat timidly, "Mommy, how come all of the presents that had tags that said, 'To: Jadie, From: Santa' were in your handwriting?'"

"Because, sweetie, Santa has so many presents stuffed into his bag that he can't put the tags on them at the North Pole because the tags would all get torn off when he was going up and down the chimneys. That's why Santa asks all the Moms and Dads to write the tags ahead of time so that when he gets to the houses he can just stick them on when he gets there. That way kids aren't opening the wrong presents, and Santa can still get around the whole world in one night," Mommy explained.

"Well why doesn't Santa just write that tags himself?" I asked.

"If he had to stop at every house and write all the tags himself he would still be delivering presents long after the sun came up. That wouldn't be any fun for little kids to wake up before their presents were there." I was relieved. Everything that Mommy said made perfect sense.

The following year in the second grade one little boy in my class said to me with a happy sneer, "Hey, Jade, did you know that there's no Santa Claus? Your parents buy your presents."

I was appalled, as were some of my classmates who were sitting at our little bank of six desks. I shot back, "Not uh, but I could believe that your Mom has to buy your presents 'cause you're so bad Santa wouldn't bring you anything anyway!"

"Yeah!" echoed two of my classmates who took solace in my defense of Father Christmas. The little boy with the big mouth looked stunned and didn't say anything else. Perhaps I made him stop and think.

It was true that Mom spent many evenings leading up to Christmas talking to Santa, which meant that Dad stayed home with Seth and I. The best part about Dad watching us was that if we behaved we could sweet talk him into letting us stay up past our bed time on a school night – something Mom would never let us get away with unless there was a Judy Garland movie on TV that we didn't have on a VHS tape, which only happened twice over the course of my childhood. Of course Seth disdained musicals so he never got to enjoy this rare privilege that Mom would grant. But Dad on the other hand was a different story. Even at this tender age we knew how to work the system. When we wanted to stay up late or eat junk food, we asked Dad. If we wanted money we asked Mom. This was true all throughout our growing up years.

One night while Mom was out talking to Santa, Seth and I did a little talking of our own and got Dad to let us stay up late to watch George C. Scott's version of *A Christmas Carol*. Seth and I had already seen Disney's *Mickey's Christmas Carol* and *Mr. Magoo's Christmas Carol* and I was interested in seeing a version of Dickens' famous tale with real people. It was interesting, up until the part when Jacob Marley's ghost appeared. I knew that there were no such things as ghosts, but Marley looked and acted so creepy that it was starting to freak me out a little bit. Dad must have noticed because he asked me, "This isn't getting you all spooked out, is it?"

"No," I squeaked out in what was barely more than a frightened whisper. I wasn't going to be dumb enough to say 'yes' and get sent to bed, especially with Jacob Marley's ghastly face so fresh in my eight-year-old mind. Even so, he sent us to bed before the movie ended anyway because it wasn't over until pretty late.

Marley's ghost may have slightly creeped me out, but my worst Christmas stress was caused by a certain relative: Uncle Shawn. He never missed an opportunity to turn my Christmas cheer into Christmas fear. This began when I was at the tender age of three. Shawn could be such a brat at times, but the fact that he has always been very intelligent and creative took the realm of his tormenting capabilities to a stratospheric level. I knew that Santa came down the chimney and through the fireplace in most houses, but when I was three we moved into a house that didn't have a fireplace, but I had never lived in a house with a fireplace so I didn't think anything about it. On Christmas Eve my Mom's entire family would get together at Gram Harman's house for a dinner. I vividly remember one particular Christmas Eve when I was three. I was standing in front of the roaring fireplace when Uncle Shawn, who was twelve, walked up to me and said, "Hey, Jadie, guess who I saw at the mall today?"

I could tell by the look on his face and the tone in his voice that trouble wasn't far behind. Still, I asked, "Who?"

"Santa Claus," said Uncle Shawn with a small grin that was beginning to curl around the corners of his mouth, "and do you know what he told me?"

"What?" I was intrigued.

"He said that since your house doesn't have a fireplace he can't get in to leave you any presents. So he's just going to leave all your presents here at my house," he reported. I was concerned. Since we had moved into a house across the street a few months ago it would be our first Christmas there and Santa hadn't been there before. I guessed that going across the street to get my presents wouldn't be so bad, but I was disappointed that Santa couldn't get into my house to leave my presents under my tree.

"But guess what?" Shawn continued, as his Grinch-like smile spread further across his smirking face, "I'm going to get a whole bunch of wrapping paper and tape and cover the front of the fireplace, and then I'm going to get a whole bunch of boards and nail them up so Santa can't get through and *you* won't get any toys!"

I was horrified! No presents! I had no doubt that my bratty Uncle Shawn was capable of such a heinous plan to keep a sweet little three year old girl, who had behaved all year long, from getting her Christmas presents from Santa. I felt my little brown eyes well up with tears and said, "But you won't get any toys either!" I protested.

Shawn just smiled and said, "I don't care because I'm a big boy and I don't play with toys." He had a point. It was true, he didn't play with toys. He was too busy playing Atari to be bothered with things as trivial as toys.

I knew I couldn't stop Shawn from carrying out his atrocious plot, so there was only one thing I could think to do. I would have to tell Mommy, and she would tell Gram, who would make Shawn behave. I knew that Gram would want me to get all the presents that Santa had for me, that were probably being put into his toy bag by the elves at that very moment. Gram wouldn't let Shawn do such a horrible thing.

I ran to Mommy and blurted out, "Mommy, Shawn said that he saw Santa at the mall and Santa said since we didn't have a fireplace he'd leave all my presents here but Shawn said he would nail boards to the fireplace so Santa couldn't get in and so I can't get any presents." I was holding back tears.

Mommy gave me a hug and said, "Now why are you listening to your Uncle Shawn? He's full of baloney. He's teasing you because Santa has a set of magic keys that can open up the lock on any door. Santa will just bring your presents into the house through the front door."

Hooray! I was relieved. I would be getting presents after all! I should have known that Mommy would be able to figure something out. She asked, "Do you know what I think?"

"What?" I asked.

"I think that Santa Claus might have to leave Shawn some coal in his stocking for telling you that. Maybe he will be the one who won't be getting any presents tomorrow," Mom smiled, and I smiled back, thrilled at the prospect. So I guess no one can really blame me when I say that the fact that Shawn did get lots of presents the next day did leave me mildly disappointed. Was there no justice? But Santa had brought me tons of cool things so it did turn out to be a very good Christmas after all.

Another Christmas that I can vividly remember Shawn attempting to inflict grief and strife upon me occurred when I was a five, which would have made him fourteen. All these years later I can still see him standing by the kitchen table, his friend Mike sitting nearby. Mike was always really nice to me, but unfortunately Shawn didn't cave to that type of peer pressure. Shawn said, "Guess what? We have a class in high school called Wood Shop where we make things out of wood."

By this point in my life I was old enough and wise enough to know that I couldn't believe everything Shawn told me, so I answered this ludicrous claim with, "Not Uh."

"Yes we do!" Shawn snapped back, obviously offended by my lack of faith in his words. He said it so convincingly I believed him. "Anyway," he resumed in a

65

kind tone of voice, "I think that you are a big enough girl for me to let you in on a little Christmas secret. I made a special Christmas present for your Mom in shop class." Something wasn't adding up. He was never this nice to me. Shawn asked, "Do you want to know what I made for your Mom?"

"What?" I asked. Maybe he had turned over a new leaf and was going to be kind to me.

His eyes widened and his nasty grin grew as he gleefully announced, "I made her a great big wooden paddle to spank you with!"

Oh the fear and horror that leapt through me with those terrible words! Shawn must have seen the distress on my face because he added, "It's about two or three inches thick, and I drilled holes in it so she could swing it faster so it would hurt more! I even put a whole bunch of nails and screws in it, too!"

"Don't give it to her!" I demanded, standing my ground as bravely as I could.

"I will, and I bet she's really going to like it. I bet she won't even want to wait for you to do something bad. She'll probably just try it out right away!" He smiled at me, his fiery red hair framing his beaming face.

This disastrous news was too much to take. I fled the kitchen and stood in front of Gram's Christmas tree that had the giant, colored antique lights on them. There were candy canes and all of the ornaments on the live pine tree that provided a festive atmosphere to Gram's beautiful Victorian home. But I just stood in front of the tree, fighting back tears and trying to figure out what to do

66

next. I wanted to tell Mommy, but Uncle Shawn said it was a Christmas secret so how could I say anything? It would ruin the surprise, as horrendous as the surprise may be.

About that time Mommy came strolling through the living room where I was trying to dismantle Shawn's tale of Christmas terror from a logical perspective, hoping to find some flaw in what he said to make this nightmare go away. I guess Mom was surprised to find me in the dark room, with only the fire in the fireplace and the lights of the tree providing any illumination. "What are you doing out here all by your lonesome, honey?" she asked.

"Mommy," I began as bravely as I could, "Shawn said that in high school there's a class called shop where they make things out of wood. Is that true?"

"Yeah, high school kids learn how to make all kinds of neat things," she said.

So it was true! There really was such a thing as 'Wood Shop' after all! She saw that I was obviously concerned and said, "What's wrong?"

"It's kind of a secret."

"Well, I can't help you if you won't tell me. I would certainly hope that you would tell me something if it was making you upset," Mommy said.

"Shawn said he made you a present there," I began cautiously.

"Well, that's nice if he did, but why do you look so worried about it?"

"Because it's not a nice present," I answered reluctantly.

"What would he make me that isn't nice?" she asked.

"I'm not allowed to tell because it's a Christmas secret."

"Well I think you better tell me if it's something that isn't good," she said.

"Shawn said he made you a big paddle to spank me with and it has sharp nails and holes so you could swing it faster," I admitted slowly, hoping that I wasn't doing something bad by not keeping Shawn's secret.

Mom hugged me and asked, "Would Mommy ever spank you with a paddle like that?"

"No," I said, and suddenly realized how ridiculous the whole thing sounded. I should have known that all along that Mommy wouldn't use a paddle like that, but Shawn always made quite a convincing argument.

"That's right; I would never, ever do something like that. I think Shawn was just teasing about the paddle though. I don't really think he actually made one."

"I think he did," I said. After all he was that mean and I bet if he thought that there was the slightest iota of possibility that she would use a paddle like that I had no doubt he would make one for her.

Mommy nodded thoughtfully. "I'll make you a deal. If Shawn really did make me a paddle, I'll give him a great big spanking with it for making you so worried. How about that?" she smiled.

"Okay!" I was overjoyed. Now I was wishing really hard that Shawn did make the paddle. He deserved a big spanking, or so I thought. Nobody ever mentioned the paddle again, so I'm guessing that he never made one in the first place. Either that or he overheard my Mom's threat and got so scared he got rid of the paddle. He probably either burned it up in the fireplace or threw it in the river.

Besides getting presents from Santa, I got presents from Mom's family too. One year Aunt Kelly got me a set of Sesame Street Weebles, which stands out in my mind as one of the coolest toys of my childhood. It came with a set of playground equipment, and I used to love to sit all the Weebles on the merry-go-round and spin it as fast as I could and watch all the little Weebles fly off and scatter in all directions. It really was true that Weebles wobbled but didn't fall down, but that never stopped me from trying to disprove the claims of the commercial.

We would celebrate New Year's at Uncle Jim and Aunt Brenda's house and we would ring in the New Year with tons of junk food and hours of Trivial Pursuit. Most of the family would eat saur kraut, pork, and mashed potatoes but I flatly refused to eat saur kraut or anything that was saturated with saur kraut brine. I didn't like the way it smelled. To this day I still have never eaten saur kraut, even though my Mom always teases me and says, "I can't believe you have the nerve to call yourself Pennsylvania Dutch when you don't eat kraut." But even though I didn't eat saur kraut, there was plenty to eat. Jim and Brenda always bought a pack of hot dogs and cooked

69

them for their nieces and nephews who weren't fans of saur kraut. Besides, there were always tons of side dishes, like Aunt Kelly's pumpernickel bread and spinach dip, as well as Christmas cookies, Middleswarth Chips (two giant bags called "Weekenders", one Bar-B-Que and one Regular, are a necessity at all of our family get-togethers), M&Ms, brownies, and about forty different types of soda. I always loved it when Gram Harman brought iced tea. She had a sweet tooth that was nothing less than legendary and she put so much sugar in her iced tea it was like drinking liquefied candy. It was truly amazing and had to be tasted to be believed.

I loved going to Harman get-togethers (or Shindigs, as Gram called them) and we had them all the time for every holiday and birthday and from time to time we would have one simply because it had been awhile since the last one. New Year's Eve was a good opportunity to bring new board games that we had been given for Christmas, and Seth and I, along with our cousins, would bring some of our new Christmas toys to play with. But even as a child, my favorite ritual of New Year's Eve can be summed up in two words: Trivial Pursuit. That was the greatest board game of the 1980s and our family played that game with steadfast devotion. I always wanted to play and was fascinated as I watched the grownups clustered around the board, intense in their concentration as they answered what I thought were impossible questions about 19th century geography and the finer points of colonial American history. There were questions about the natural sciences, sports, history, geography, arts and entertainment, and literature. As a child I was convinced that the grownups in my family were the smartest people in the whole world. Looking back, I think as a collective whole they probably were sharper than

70

most of the average population. But my Gram was brilliant, she had an excellent memory for facts and loved to read and since intelligence is the result of genetic predisposition it's not surprising that her kids turned out the same way.

I always wanted to play Trivial Pursuit, but most of my family said I wasn't allowed to because I was too little. Truthfully I didn't really know the answers to any of the questions, but there was always one person who would overlook my young age and lack of knowledge: Uncle Jim. Uncle Jim and Aunt Brenda didn't have any children of their own so Uncle Jim always went out of his way to treat his nieces and nephews like gold. A lot of times the minute he arrived at family get-togethers that he didn't have at his own house, one of us kids would excitedly yell, "Jim's here!" and we would all run over to him to give him hugs. Before the day was over most of us would always ask him to play games and tell us stories. I can't ever remember him refusing.

Uncle Jim saw my enthusiasm to play Trivial Pursuit and would always make it a point to ask me if I would be on his team and roll the die. He made me feel like I had some sort of special gift for rolling die and his team would surely face defeat if I were not there to help him out and lead them to victory. Jim was so enthusiastic when I landed on a wedge or on a "Roll Again," space he would thank and congratulate me so profusely that it would be a few years before I realized that my die rolling skills were no different than anyone else's. Interestingly, as the years went on I did become quite the Trivial Pursuit player. I couldn't really actively contribute to the team until I was about twelve, but I'm still on Jim's team whenever we play so his kind investment in letting me join the game did end up providing a good return. In my family I'm a good Trivial Pursuit player. Outside of my family I take all comers and usually intellectually annihilate any challengers (notice that I said usually, not always). The 1980s may be long over but the original Trivial Pursuit Genus Edition is just as popular as it ever was in my family.

After the New Year would arrive we would get together with my Dad's side of the family at the house of his father and step-mother, Papa Heasley and Grandma Deb. We always got together after Christmas because Papa and Grandma Deb were both professors at Penn State University and with their busy schedules it was easier to get together in January. Seth and I always looked forward to seeing our great-grandmother, Grammy Heasley, our grandparents, cousins Jason, Eric, and Benjie, and aunts and uncles, Cheryl and Merle, Paul and Barb, and Scott and Patty. We would eat lasagna for dinner and open gifts. Grammy Heasley loved having all of her family together for this annual event. She made enough cookies to feed most of the Western Hemisphere and she always sent each individual family home with dozens of cookies. Traveling to Papa and Grandma's house felt like it took all day, though in reality it was less than an hour-and-a-half, but the trip home always flew because we ate Grammy's cookies and had new toys to play with.

The worst part of Christmas vacation was having it come to an end. Going back to school was an absolute drag. At least in elementary school we usually had show-and-tell, which may as well have been called "show off-and-brag." Every kid was convinced that they had gotten the coolest Christmas toy, and it was fun to show off a new toy and see what the other kids got. But the best part about going back to school in January was the possibility of a snow day.

Snow Days: The Best Days of the School Year

Growing up in Pennsylvania meant that we usually had a white Christmas, but every few years we had a green Christmas as well. Regardless of what color Christmas was, January was always white and icy and sleety and eventually turned varying ugly shades of dark gray from cinders and road dirt splattered on the once white snow. Every time the sky began to fill with opaque gray clouds I would anxiously watch the skies in anticipation for falling snow, hoping that it would accumulate enough for the powers that be in the school district to deem the roads too dangerous for travel and shut down the school. True, two-hour delays were always fun but nothing was better than a snow day.

Since Mom was a stay-at-home-mom she was always ready to do something fun on a snow day. She would bundle me up in my gray snow suit and boots, along with a hat, scarf, earmuffs and mittens, until I bore a striking resemblance to Randy from *A Christmas Story*. Mom would help us build snowmen and once she really impressed me by building a snow horse that was big enough for Seth and I to sit on. But our yard was as flat as sheet of paper so if we wanted to go sled riding she would take us to Gram's house, which had a hill down the side yard that seemed to stretch out a mile long. Gram was always more than happy to let us ride our sleds in her yard, putting sled tracks all the way down the hill and stamping our boot tracks the whole way back up. Seth and I took the red plastic saucer sleds that Santa brought us, but if we were joined by Uncle Shawn (who mysteriously behaved when Mom or Gram was around) or Aunt Kelly and her son, Bo, we would take turns riding each other's sleds. We would ride our sleds for quite some time, until Mom would make us go home after being outside awhile, which we usually didn't want to do. Mom had heard some crazy rumor that you shouldn't let small children go outside in freezing temperatures for hours on end and she believed it, unfortunately.

Once we were back at home Mom made hot cocoa to warm us up while lunch was cooking, which was often Mrs. Grass Soup and grilled cheese sandwiches. After lunch we were allowed to do what we wanted, such as play with toys or watch TV. Sometimes Mom would read to us during these long, gray afternoons. This eventually turned into the habit of reading to us from Laura Ingalls Wilder's *Little House on the Prairie* books, and over time she read us the entire series.

It was fun to ride sleds during the day, but going sled riding at night was ten times more fun. Mom, Dad, Seth, my aunts, uncles, and cousins would gather and take turns flying down the hill, riding in saucer sleds, inflatable snow tubes, and wooden runner sleds with metal runners that had a fresh coat of wax. The lampposts across the street would provide plenty of light for these nights of sled riding adventures in a frozen utopia of winter joy. Once we sailed down the hill we would begin the long trek back up the hill, staying off to the side so that oncoming sleds wouldn't collide with us. The hill towered so largely in front of us it seemed like Gram owned her own mountain. Since I was usually the oldest cousin at these nighttime sled riding events I could be counted on to take my little cousin Bo down the hill. He was six years younger than me and I remember sitting on the back of a plastic sled, Bo sitting in front of me, while I held on to him and a grownup gave us a big push down the hill. We did this often, but I can remember once when the sled seemed to be going faster than it normally did and was headed right for the giant pine tree and the telephone pole that were usually far beyond the range of our sleds. Fearing a crash, I hung onto Bo as tightly as I could and bailed off the sled's left side. We tumbled into the thick frozen snow and Bo looked at me wide-eyed and asked, "Why did you do that?"

"I didn't want us to crash into the tree," I explained while helping him get back up on his feet.

"Why not?" Bo asked. The toddler was too innocent and oblivious in the ways of the world to realize the obvious dangers of smashing small human beings into tree trunks and telephone poles.

"Because we would have gotten hurt," I told him sagely, feeling mature beyond my years in dispensing such a grand pearl of wisdom.

"Oh," he answered, satisfied by my sensible explanation. I remember that I looked over at the plastic sled and saw that it went between the tree and pole, which were about four or five feet apart. Escaping the sled had caused the sled to shift in its course, but I couldn't help but wonder if we hadn't have bailed if we would have hit the tree. Of course we might have stayed on the sled and not hit the tree or the telephone pole. Another point that I didn't realize until years later was that both of us were so bundled up in about seventy layers of winter clothes that had we crashed the tree or the pole probably would have suffered more damage than we would have. I guess my actions that day could either be considered heroic or spastic. I'm not sure which so I will allow you to draw your own conclusion.

Ha! Ha! Ha! Look at Those Clothes!

I remember sitting on the stylish brown and tan plaid sofa bed looking at the "old" photograph albums that my Mom kept during her and my Dad's dating years. I would laugh at the pictures from the late 1970s, my childish giggles usually punctuated with "Ha! Ha! Ha! Look at Mommy's clothes! Ha! Ha! Ha! Look at Daddy's hair!" The sight of my Mom in bellbottoms and my Dad with his Greg Brady haircut cracked me up to no end.

"Go ahead and laugh, Jadie, but your Dad and I were really in style for the time," Mom said, "and I guarantee you that bellbottoms will come back in style."

"No way!" I'd say in disbelief. The "old" Polaroid pictures of my parents made them look like they could be the first runners-up of a Donny and Marie look-a-like contest (Dad's Burt Reynolds-style mustache would have cost them). I'd be sitting there in my giant oversized sweater with massive shoulder pads and tight stonewashed jeans refusing to think that those fashion monstrosities of polyester bellbottoms and equally tacky tops from the 1970s would ever come back in style.

"That stuff will all come back in style, you wait and see. I bet that they will come back in before you graduate high school and you'll be wearing them," she said with a knowing smile.

"No way, even if they do come in I won't be wearing bellbottoms," I informed her matter-of-factly.

"Yes you will," she taunted me.

Sure enough, Mom was right. When I was in high school bellbottoms, appearing under the alias of "boot cut," had made their way back into the inner circle of fashion. But a strange thing had happened. All of the 1980s clothing that I had worn as a child had fallen *out* of fashion. Now my cousin Karman, who wasn't even born until well into the 1990s, teases me good naturedly about my elementary school outfits. She would proudly describe in detail, while doubling over, the outfit that D.J. Tanner had worn on the last *Full House* rerun she had seen and conclude with, "My Mom said you had an outfit that was almost exactly like it."

One trend from the 1980s that I was thrilled to see come to an end was the side ponytail. Mom, on the other hand thought it was adorable so I didn't have a lot of choice in the matter. The reason I hated the side ponytail was because it made my head feel off balance. Any other hairdo was fine, but it was the side ponytail that was the worst of the 1980s hair styles that I had to endure.

The Day I Discovered Telephone Books and Long Distance Phone Calls

The 1980s were an amazing time for telephone technology. I think everyone remembers being in awe the first time they saw a cordless phone, I know I was. My Aunt Kelly had one. It was a push button, touchtone phone that was tan and weighed about eight pounds. The antenna pulled out to an impressive four feet and on a good day you could walk as far as three feet from the phone's base before the signal broke up with static. If you were lucky, you could even pick up someone else's conversation. The only bad part about cordless phones was that you had to remember to stay several feet away from the wall while you were using them. This was due to the length of the antenna; if you turned your head to the side you risked scraping the antenna across the wall and knocking all the pictures and glass sconces off the wall (glass sconces were often incorporated into classy décor during this era, at least for the middle class).

One impressive phone incident that stands out in my mind occurred in my Gram Harman's kitchen. She had recently switched from a rotary dial to a touchtone phone and I was intrigued. The smooth sounding and easy to operate touchtone phone was quite the improvement over the clickity-clacking spinning rotary dial. Gram was babysitting me that spring day and I was sitting near the phone when I saw her put a thick paperback book into one of her kitchen drawers. Since she had a book shelf in the living room I was wondering why this one was relegated to being hidden away in a drawer full of odds and ends. When I questioned her on this point she told me that it wasn't a regular book, it was a phone book. Being intensely curious I wanted to know more, and she explained to me the brilliant concept of alphabetizing all the names of people and businesses in one convenient book that provided the phone numbers to contact them. I was fascinated by the long, long lists of numbers. Each page consisted of multiple lists, and the phone book was several hundred pages thick. How did they come up with all those numbers?

I was so intrigued by the phone book that I couldn't get it off my mind, although I'm not sure why because my parents provided me with plenty of toys and books to keep me occupied. I concluded that eventually the phone company was going to run out of numbers and I wanted to help them avoid this tragedy. I decided that I was going to help the phone company by inventing new phone numbers.

After I was alone in the kitchen I sat down on the radiator that was underneath the phone and took the plastic receiver in my benevolent five-year-old hand. I began pressing random numbers. I didn't bother with area codes or local exchanges; I just happily went about pushing the buttons until I heard something in the receiver. Most of what I got were pre-recorded messages saying that the number I had dialed was not working or was no longer in service. Every once in awhile I would get a busy signal, and sometimes people would pick up and say, "Hello?" I just hung up on them because it was dangerous and bad to talk to strangers. Besides, the fact that someone answered the phone meant that the phone company had already discovered that number. Part way through this process I toyed with the idea of writing down the numbers that I had discovered, but I ruled against it because I didn't want to be bothered. I can't remember what I thought the criteria for a newly discovered number would be, but my lack of practical knowledge of what exactly I was looking for didn't stop me in my noble numeric quest.

I'm not sure how long I sat out in the kitchen pushing buttons, but I remember getting busted. Mom strolled into the kitchen after returning from wherever she was and said, "What are you doing on Gram's phone?" I could tell by the look that I got that I was doing something that I shouldn't be.

"I wanted to make up new phone numbers," I said truthfully. It made perfect sense to me.

"Well make up new phone numbers on paper, not on the real phone. Were you talking to someone?" she asked.

"No," which was true because I never said a word to anyone.

That was the end of the incident, or so I thought. I never realized the significance of that day until many years later. When I was in my early twenties we had a picnic at our house and most of my Mom's extended family was in attendance. We were taking turns sharing happy memories of bratty things we had done when we were little and I told my Gram that I had used her phone to try to invent some new phone numbers. My Gram's jaw dropped. "I remember that! I got a phone bill that had all these really weird toll calls and I had no idea what they were. I just blamed it on Shawn. He swore up and down it wasn't him but I never believed him." Since I always behaved for Gram she just laughed the whole thing off.

"I'm sorry, Gram. I hope I didn't run your phone bill up," I apologized, still laughing.

"Oh no, Jadie, none of them were for any length of time, just a lot of weird numbers," she chuckled.

Mom said, "Well, Jade, at least you got Shawn in trouble. You only owed him about a million for all the times he picked on you."

"I know," I laughed.

By anyone's standard I probably still do owe my Uncle Shawn a certain amount of revenge, but fortunately I have a good sense of humor and can laugh at and appreciate his subtle bratty teenage genius for tormenting small children. But at the time his antics were no laughing matter.

So if you remember getting a hang-up phone call in the mid-1980s it may have been me. I can't say for sure though. But I can tell you that wasn't E.T. phoning your home.

Water Battle Fun

Seth was the proud owner of a Slip 'n Slide. The bright yellow plastic sheet that sprayed water was responsible for hours of fun during my childhood. The same hill at Gram's house that was perfect for sled riding was also great for the Slip 'n Slide. Gram Harman was more than happy to let her grandkids come over to her house, hook up her garden hose to the Slip 'n Slide for two hours of continuous use and create a massive mud puddle as a result. She never minded. Let me just take a moment to say that I am not advising that you use a Slip 'n Slide down a hill, always follow the manufacturer's instructions for safe use.

The Slip 'n Slide wasn't the only fun thing that we did that was water related. Mom would let us have squirt gun battles and water balloon fights in our back yard. She bought us a plastic dishwashing tub for the sole purpose of filling it with water to fill our squirt guns. Mom would also volunteer to (or rather insist that she alone) fill the water balloons, and each of us got the same number of balloons to throw at each other. I remember when my older cousin Jason came over to play one time and he brought a package of water balloon grenades, which was the first time that I had ever seen them. The green balloons had a grid pattern stamped into them and looked a lot like real grenades. These water balloon grenades seemed to have a lot more splatter power to them than regular water balloons. I thought that they were the coolest water toys ever invented. Mom didn't mind our throwing water balloons around, just as long as we went through the yard afterward and painstakingly picked up every single piece of broken balloon when we were finished. That was a tough job.

Of course there were days when the heat and humidity was so stifling that getting sprayed by a squirt gun wasn't adequate to prevent heat stroke. Days like this called for swimming, and once we had outgrown kiddy pools in the backyard Mom would take us to either one of two public pools in the surrounding towns. One time when I was around six-years-old Mom said that she was going to take me and Seth to the pool, which was always fun. They even had a snack bar where Mom would let us each pick out a treat. I was excited to go and spend the afternoon splashing around, and by this point I was big enough to swim underwater with my eyes open – a feat of phenomenal skill that I was quite proud of. I was such a good swimmer that I didn't need to take any baby things along like inner tubes or arm floaties or rafts, but Seth had to because he was only two and needed something to keep him occupied in the baby pool. I couldn't wait to go, but then at the last minute Mom decided it would be nice of her to offer to take her fifteen-year-old brother along. We stopped at Gram's house to pick up Uncle Shawn, and Mom went into the kitchen to talk to Gram for a minute. I was standing in the living room when Shawn gave me his infamous "I'm Plotting Something Bratty" smile and announced triumphantly, "Guess what, Jade? When we get to the pool I'm going to stick your head in the filter!"

"No!" I insisted, terrified at the thought of being trapped in a swimming pool filter, barely able to keep my face above the water line and having chlorine perpetually burn my eyes. I had seen the pool filter, the big square hole with a plastic door that was constantly snapping open and shut and made all those scary, sloshing noises. The thought of being trapped in it really shook me up.

"Yes I am!" Shawn smiled. "They'll never be able to get you out either. Not unless they cut off your head, so you'll just have to be stuck there forever until you're an old lady."

I was scared! Going to the pool was such a fun thing to do, but I knew that if Mom asked Shawn to go he would find some way to ruin it. It didn't help matters any that on the four mile car ride to the pool Shawn and I were sitting in the backseat and I looked over at him and once again he flashed his "I'm Plotting Something Bratty" smile at me, something that I had come to know well over the years. He had me convinced that he really was going to carry out his threat. Fortunately he left me alone, but whether it's because he took pity on me and decided to be merciful or he got too distracted checking out the teenage girls in bikinis isn't something that I can answer. But I have to admit I was careful to stay close to Mommy on that particular trip.

The best memories of summer water fun occurred after Mom and Dad bought an aboveground pool. It was three feet deep and twelve feet across, but looking back it seems impossible that the pool was that small. We had all sorts of pool toys, rafts, and diving rings. By this point Aunt Kelly, her husband, and son, Bo lived next door to us, and Kelly and Bo would come over nearly every day to swim during the summer. Kelly was a stay-at-home-mom just like Mom. We would all eat lunch together in our back yard and basically had a picnic every afternoon. Mom would make peanut butter and jelly sandwiches and Kool-Aid for Seth, Bo, and I, and Kelly made her own lunchtime contribution to our feast thanks to a mysterious high-tech appliance called a microwave oven. Every day she would make a bag of microwave popcorn and I remember being astounded by it. Her six hundred dollar microwave was a huge metal box that could cook nearly anything in a matter of mere minutes. Kelly would get a pre-packaged bag of microwave popcorn that already had salt and butter mixed in, and in a few minutes the microwave would pop all the popcorn kernels and have them buttered and salted. This was quite different from Mom and Dad's popcorn maker which was transparent yellow plastic and required Mom to pour in the oil and popcorn seeds into the popcorn popper and chop up a stick of butter to melt in the small plastic pan on top of the popper. Then we would have to wait about ten minutes for the machine to get heated up enough to pop the popcorn. After that Mom had to dump the melted butter on the popcorn and mix it up and add salt. But somehow Kelly's microwave was able to reduce the seemingly complicated popcorn popping process into a few button pushes to produce perfect popcorn in three minutes. That popcorn had enough butter and salt on it to kill a small horse and we loved it. It was almost exactly like the popcorn at the movies.

Those afternoons were lots of fun and we kids enjoyed playing in the pool. However, Mom and Kelly would often opt to skip the pool altogether to lie on their plastic reclining lawn chairs and get suntans. The dark tans that they could get were a nice way to highlight their fashionable plastic earrings and humongous big bangs. From time to time they would each get a bucket of water to pat some water on their skin, but a lot of times I would volunteer to lightly pour water on them instead. More than once I "accidentally" dumped the whole bucket of cold water on them. When Mom got angry it just made the situation funnier. In all honesty, the volunteering was pre-planned to include a mishap with the bucket. Being bratty was a source of so much joy! But there was a reason for this: since they were already soaked they would just simply take the plunge and get in the pool. Once they were in we would usually get a gigantic whirlpool going, which was always fun. Once the circular current was fully established I liked to hop in an inner tube or float on a mini-raft and let the water pull me around in circles. Those perfect summer days seemed like they would go on forever. How little did we realize that we were being catapulted through time more quickly than any of us could have ever imagined.

Mom vs. Music Videos

MTV made its debut on August 1, 1981, a few days shy of my first birthday. I can remember watching MTV once I got a little bit older, but obviously I don't remember the earliest days of when it hit the air waves. I usually did my MTV watching at Gram's house because my Uncle Shawn watched it incessantly, usually with a glass bottle of soda and a bag of Middleswarth BBQ chips in hand. A few years after MTV premiered, on January 1, 1985, VH1 was unleashed upon the world. At our house we watched both networks and between the two I can remember seeing all the 1980s classic music videos such as Bon Jovi's "Runaway," "Livin' On a Prayer," and "You Give Love a Bad Name," Toni Basil's "Mickey," Swing Out Sister's "Break Out," Gloria Estefan and Miami Sound Machine's "Rhythm is Gonna Get You," Billy Joel's "We Didn't Start the Fire," Nena's "99 Luftballoons," Cyndi Lauper's, "Girls Just Wanna Have Fun," Van Halen's "Jump," and Jefferson Starship's "Nothing's Gonna Stop Us Now," among others. These videos were all good, and most of them were a far cry from some of the earlier music videos which basically consisted of filming a band playing on a stage with a few changes in camera angle now and then. By the mid-1980s music videos had gotten a lot more impressive. One of the most memorable music videos from this era is The Bangles' "Walk Like an Egyptian" which featured everyone from waitresses to mullet wielding businessmen walking like Egyptians. I thought it was so cool when they featured Princess Diana and even the Statue of Liberty walking like Egyptians! What's even funnier is that the special effects looked really real at the time. That is still one of my favorite music videos.

No one who lived through this era could forget watching Michael Jackson's "Thriller," which seemed like a really long video, years later I would find out the original run time was almost fourteen minutes and even included a full set of credits at the end. I was pretty young when "Thriller" came out and even though it was creepy enough to scare me just a little bit, particularly where Michael Jackson has scary eyes at the end of the video, I just had to watch it. Looking back I think that part of my reason for watching it was just to prove I wasn't too scared to watch it. I think the reason that I could handle watching "Thriller" was because thanks to Mommy I was far too sensible a child to believe in things like monsters, zombies or ghosts. Secondly, even if those creatures really did exist all that they would be doing would be following Michael Jackson down the street break dancing in perfect formation, as opposed to chasing people through darkened forests. Michael Jackson would go on to have lots of other famous videos, but I think that everyone was impressed by the hilarious genius who made fun of Michael's videos, Weird Al Yankovic. Weird Al did a lot of entertaining spoofs in that era, but probably his most famous was "Fat," to the tune of Michael Jackson's "Bad." I think that everyone in my elementary school knew every line of Weird Al's masterpiece. I remember gleefully singing it with members of my soccer team, and I do believe those occasions were the only time I have ever sang in public voluntarily (at least outside of church).

One day Mom told me that we weren't going to be watching MTV anymore. But I wanted my MTV! Mom had seen one particular music video and felt that an image in it was sacrilegious and decided that was enough. I wasn't happy, and I admit that I would try to "sneak" watching MTV at Gram's house while Shawn was watching it, but this was often tinged with guilt for not listening to Mommy. I sort of tried to reason that MTV wasn't allowed at *our* house and I wasn't watching it at *our* house. Mom knew I was upset that MTV wasn't an option for our house anymore, but consoled me by saying that VH1 was still okay. I remember sitting in front of our state of the art, large, wooden Zenith floor model television and watching VH1. The Zenith was really modern because all of the controls were buttons rather than knobs. It's funny to look back and realize that as high-tech as the television was it didn't have a remote control. But it did have a VCR sitting on top (which did have a remote control), and on top of the VCR sat a cable box with about thirty buttons. It always kind of mystified me that the wood grain cable box had more buttons than we had TV channels.

When I watched VH1 I had my tape recorder sitting beside me so I could record the cool songs. Dad's mother, my Grandma Annette, had bought me the tape recorder as a gift and I loved to play and record music on it. That tape player was a yellowish tan color with dark brown accents, it had a power switch, a fast forward button, a rewind button, a play button, a record button, and a stop/eject button. It weighed about twelve pounds but it worked and I loved it. I remember one tape had "Break Out" on it about six times. I loved that song.

I saw tons of great videos during this era but one stands out in my mind as my personal favorite is "Take On Me" by a-ha. Who could forget the classic video where they combined cartoon animation with live action footage? I was astonished at how much the cartoon people looked just like the real people, especially when they kept changing back and forth from real people to cartoons. As a pop song, "Take On Me" was catchy, but the video put it over the top. Who can forget the suspenseful ending of the handsome comic book hero throwing himself against the walls in a desperate attempt to rid himself of his animated existence? A lot of things that were filmed in the 1980s that feature special effects look cheesy by today's standards, but this video is every bit as incredible as when it first came out. I don't know who came up with the concept of that video, but they deserve a massive award for their brilliance.

One thing that I have noticed is that about once every seven to ten years a group from Northern Europe becomes enormously successful in the realm of U.S. pop music. That might not sound like the most astute observation, but isn't it curious that the names of the bands all start with the letter "A"? Don't believe me? This started in the 1970s with ABBA, happened again in the 1980s with a-ha, and occurred twice in the 1990s with Ace of Base and later with Aqua. Weird, huh?

My First 45

One year during the mid-1980s Dad bought Mom a huge, top of the line Pioneer stereo system for Christmas. She was ecstatic and liked it even better than the black and white TV he had bought her for their bedroom on her birthday (this was a time when owning two televisions was somewhat of an extravagance). The stereo was a huge black metal and plastic framed device with great big speakers that were padded with foam. The stereo had a record player, a tape deck, and an AM/FM radio. We played cassettes on the stereo but mostly we played records. Dad had accumulated a big collection of records that began in his bachelor days that included a lot of albums by Billy Joel and Bruce Springsteen. By the time that *Born in the U.S.A.* was released we were technologically advanced enough to buy the cassette rather than the record, and we nearly wore the tape out. Cassettes were great because you could play them in the house or in the car. But we still bought record albums frequently. Mom had a number of records, but out of all her records one of my favorites was *Sports* by Huey Lewis and the News. Aunt Kelly had given it to Mom for her birthday and we listened to it constantly. The album had "Heart of Rock and Roll" on it and it was interesting because the song would start out with a solo bass drum. As soon as this song began no matter what Seth was doing he would immediately stop whatever he was doing and jump up and run in circles, completely oblivious to his surroundings. Seth was about two or three-years-old and did this every time and sometimes Mom would specifically play that song just to watch his reaction. None of us knew why and Seth never offered an explanation, although Mom always asked him about it he refused to give her an answer. Once he reached adulthood he told us that he had faint recollections of thinking that a dinosaur was coming and it scared the daylights out of him. Although how running in circles was supposed to keep an approaching dinosaur from attacking is beyond me; but who am I to question the logic of toddler?

After Mom got the stereo I remember her taking us to buy some 45 records. We went to Hill's Department Store or to a local record shop. Mom would carefully flip through the records that came in the paper sleeves, reading us song titles and artists. She would usually buy two or three 45s at a time. Once we were home I couldn't wait to hear the new records. We had The Go Gos' "We Got the Beat," and The Bangles' "Walk Like an Egyptian," which was one of my favorite songs. We also had The Bangles' single, "Manic Monday." Mom loved to turn the stereo up pretty loud, which I thought was really cool. She would always make me laugh by showing me her repertoire of 1960s dance moves, such as The Swim, The Twist, The Skate, The Jerk, The Monkey, and The Pony. I always tried to copy her steps, and I could dance the Twist and the Swim enough to do them some minimal level of justice, but the Pony was a completely elusive enigma to me. To this day I still have never figured that one out. But my dance skills are virtually non-existent so that's no surprise to anyone who knows me or has had the tragic misfortune of seeing my attempts at dancing. But our impromptu dance parties had to be kept toned down, because if not we risked making the needle create a permanent scratch across the vinyl and rendering the record unusable.

One day when Mom pulled Bessie the Station Wagon into the driveway after picking me up from school she said, "Go upstairs to your room and see the surprise that I got for you today."

A surprise? She got me a surprise? I eagerly ran up the stairs (holding the railing, of course) to my room and saw something wonderful propped up on my footstool: John Cougar Mellancamp's 45 single of "R.O.C.K. in the U.S.A." John stood there handsomely on the record sleeve in a black and white photograph with his guitar. It was so cool! Mom knew I liked the song but now I had my own copy of it. I was so excited! This was my first real rock-and-roll record, all the other records I had were nursery rhymes, story book records, and a Kermit the Frog record featuring the song "Rainbow Connection," a song I still love to this day. But now I had a real rock-and-roll record and I was thrilled!

I remember being in awe as I took the glossy black vinyl record out from the thin paper sleeve. Sure, I could go downstairs and have Mom play it on her stereo but this was *my* record and I wanted to have the record make its premier it in *my* room, so I fired up my Show n' Tell Phono Viewer which did work as a regular record player. The analog record spun in slow circles, churning out some great rock music. This was so much cooler than the fairytale records that the Phono Viewer usually played.

I always have loved music and in adulthood would get my own stereo system that had a triple cd changer, double tape deck, AM/FM radio, record player *and* a remote control that was the envy of nearly everyone in my college dorm. I would amass quite the collection of cds and vintage vinyl albums, and then learn that there was a new type of hot music technology called an mp3 player and would eventually get an iPod Video. But no matter how technologically advanced music players become, great music lives on forever and will emerge in every format that comes out. But it doesn't matter how big your music collection becomes, you will never forget your first rock-and-roll record.

The Golden Age of Snack Food

When I was little and we had to go the grocery store Mom always gave me the special job of picking out the Kool-Aid packets. If Mom and I were the only ones to go to the store, I got to pick out all the Kool-Aid flavors, but if Seth was along we each got to pick half of the flavors. I remember carefully choosing which packets I wanted, all of them had an identical picture of the Kool-Aid pitcher on the front, and they were color-coded according to the flavor. My favorites were Orange, Lime, Grape, and Tropical Punch. As a kid Kool-Aid always remained my favorite thing to drink, even though every time I turned on the television I was reminded, "Milk. It Does a Body Good."

Once we had the beverage choices under control I would begin my weekly campaign of asking my Mom for every type of junk food and snack food that was on the shelves. Mom had enough of a backbone to not give into my incessant questions of "Can we get that?" which is good, because if she had indulged me I probably would have dropped over dead from a sugar overdose before my seventh birthday.

I would like to state that this was probably the best age of food advertising on TV. McDonald's commercials left me with the impression that any kid having a rough day could count on Ronald McDonald to come strolling along, fix everything that was wrong in the world, and then treat everyone to cheeseburgers, French fries, and chocolate milk shakes. Usually by this time Birdie, Hamburgler, Grimace, the Fry Guys, and the Chicken McNuggets would come and join in the fun. I loved those McDonald's commercials, but they always left me with a lingering question: What it the world was Grimace? He wasn't an animal. He wasn't a monster, or at least he didn't seem to be. So what was he? To this day I still can't answer that question.

Kool-Aid Man bursting through the walls giving away Kool-Aid was always a sight that every kid wished would happen in real life. It seemed like the commercials that didn't feature Kool-Aid Man bashing through walls featured break dancing kids in wildly colored clothes. I have no idea who wrote the Kool-Aid commercials in that era but they had a gift and were able to get every kid to stop whatever it was they were doing and give their undivided attention to the television until the commercial was through.

The idea of drinking milk was never as appealing as it was in the "Milk. It Does a Body Good." commercials, particularly the one from 1985 that was more like watching a music video than a commercial. Although invisible cats, nasal telephone operators, robots, and animated kangaroos might not be the traditional images that pop into one's mind when they think of the calcium laden beverage, they all contributed to one very cool commercial.

Who could forget the break dancing boy from the Chef Boyardee Tic-Tac-Toes commercial? He was the first TV personality I had a crush on. The goal of eating Tic-Tac-Toes, besides nourishment to ward off pesky things like rickets and starvation, was to be the first to get three "X"s or "O"s on your spoon.

Cereal commercials would emphasize sugary goodness over the essential vitamins and minerals. Remember when Honey Smacks were Sugar Smacks? Most cereal commercials were cartoons, and I was always fascinated by the combination of cartoons and live action, such as Tony the Tiger selling Frosted Flakes. The voice of Tony the Tiger was none other than the legendary Thurl Ravenscroft, who was also sang "You're a Mean One, Mr. Grinch" in the cartoon classic *How the Grinch Stole Christmas!*

But as awesome as the celebration of sugar was, the best part about cereal in the 1980s can be summed up in two words: The Prize. Whenever Mom would tell me to pick out a box of cereal, she would wait until I was just about to drop the box in the cart when she would say in her loud question tone, "Are you picking that cereal out because you want to eat it or are you choosing it for the prize?" She already knew the answer.

I would respond with, "I'll eat the cereal."

"That's not what I asked," she'd say.

"I want the prize but I'll eat the cereal," I'd answer honestly, and as long as I ate whatever cereal I had chosen she didn't mind. Just for good measure I would usually tack on, "Please?" I never once remember her telling me "no" and that's probably because I always ate whatever cereal she had agreed to buy, no matter how abominable that particular cereal happened to be. If I didn't, I knew that Mom held the power to decide what cereal would be purchased in the future and I couldn't take the risk of cutting myself off from the amazing toys that were exclusively available to the consumers of certain select cereals.

One cereal that I always chose, while it was available, was called Freakies. Sadly they only made it for a few months during my childhood; it had originally appeared in the 1970s but was discontinued a few years later. But during my time they briefly re-introduced it. The sight of the Freakies characters on the box surfboarding through outer space was pretty cool. Not to mention the fact that it was called "Freakies" made it all the more cool. I must admit that if they rereleased that cereal tomorrow I'd be the first one in line at the grocery store to get a box. I can't remember any of the prizes with the exception of the hologram "medal" that you could cut from the front of the box. But as far as Freakies were concerned, I chose them for the flavor rather than the prize.

But Freakies were gone within a few months and then I went back to my habit of choosing the cereal with the best prize. Honeycomb gave out digital watches on more than one occasion in what was arguably one of the best cereal box prize giveaways ever. I had a couple of the yellow watches but sadly I couldn't seem to get my hands on a blue or red one to round out my collection. Other greats included Fruity Pebbles giving out stuffed Dino dolls, and Cap'n Crunch offering little plastic boats that you could fill with baking soda that would propel themselves around the sink, and Corn Pops gave away glow-in-the-dark Wacky Wall Walkers. I remember the thrill of pulling the Wacky Wall Walker out of the cereal box throwing it against the wall and watching it crawl down to the floor. I had a lot of fun for about two minutes until I accidentally tossed it behind the refrigerator. I was fearing that it was gone forever when my Dad, who was exhausted from his hour and a half commute to the car dealership where he stood on cement floors fixing cars all day, took pity on me and hauled the refrigerator away from the wall so I could retrieve my toy. It had some dust clinging to it but some warm water and a little bit of dish soap cleaned it right up and it was as good as new.

I remember when Teenage Mutant Ninja Turtles Cereal gave away cereal bowls that were sealed to the front of the box with clear plastic. This was awesome because you knew which character you were getting so you could make sure that you collected all four, just like the commercial suggested. I also remember when Teenage Mutant Ninja Turtle Cereal gave out mini comic books that were about the size of a playing card. I carefully dug through the cereal box on the first day of fourth grade to get the comic book and then hid it in one of the pockets of my stonewashed overalls. I knew that a significant amount of time on the first day of school would be spent reading aloud and discussing the rule book. Since I always behaved in school (well, mostly) this annual practice of reviewing school policies with a fine-toothed comb left me bored out of my head. They went over the same rules every year: no fist fights, no chewing gum, no spandex, no stealing cars from the faculty parking lot, etc. So I sat at my desk with the red covered rule book in hand, pretending to be reading along, even though I was actually reading about the radical victories of the "heroes in half shells." I must have done this convincingly because the teacher didn't catch me, and I'm guessing that none of my classmates did either because no one bothered to tattle tale on me. I feel so bad for kids nowadays since the time of every cereal box having a prize is over.

Teenage Mutant Ninja Turtles Cereal and Freakies weren't the only foods that I enjoyed from the 1980s. The geniuses at Nabisco, who brought the world the incomparable Oreo cookie, came up with Giggles cookies, sandwich cookies with happy faces (hence the name). I remember when I first saw the commercial for Giggles I thought that they were the neatest cookie any company had ever invented. The cool thing about these cookies was that the facial features were designed so that there were holes in the cookies for the eyes and the mouth to make the cream in the middle visible. Another innovation of these particular cookies was the fact that the cream was half white and half chocolate, giving the appearances that the eyes had pupils. Giggles came in a few different flavors and I was really disappointed when they stopped making them.

There were also Dooleys, a snack food that was similar to Combos. The outer crunchy shell was very much like a thick potato chip and the middle had a sour cream and onion filling. Quackers were really good cheese crackers that were shaped like ducks and had lots of salt, as I remember. There was also a short-lived corn snack called Spirals in the shape of, what else, a spiral and they were loaded with nacho cheese flavored powder. I have to say I miss some of those foods. Sadly, as time marches on it has a tendency to clear out the grocery store shelves and banish some of the best snack foods in the process.

A Shocking Trip to the Mall

During the summer Mom, Seth, and I would make our weekly pilgrimage to the mall. I liked going to the mall on the weekdays a lot better than the weekends because there were a lot less people roaming around, making the lines shorter.

In the summer I often wore neon colored jam shorts and a matching neon tank top. Looking back I must have had thousands of jam shorts and coordinating tank tops. Of course my outfit was never complete without two or three jelly bracelets, a massive pair of plastic earrings, and a coordinating plastic hair barrette the size of a cassette tape. My major concerns with going to the mall were two-fold: remembering my red plastic wallet with panda bears stamped on it that held my two or three dollars worth of allowance in it, and yelling "Front Seat!" before Seth did.

We all got into the family car, the 1979 Plymouth Volaré Station Wagon that Mom had named "Bessie" (thank goodness she gave me a much cooler name than the car). When Mom and Dad first bought the car it was a very stylish metallic brown color. Later we repainted it a chic shade of tan. As a kid the station wagon seemed huge, about twelve feet wide and at least thirty feet long.

Mom would often stop by the gas station before leaving town and spend five dollars on half a tank of gas before we drove eight miles to the only shopping mall in our area. Once I got to the mall I was really excited to go in and have fun, but I had to remember to leave the car slowly and with the greatest caution. Bessie the Station Wagon had tan vinyl seats but lacked the luxury of an air-conditioner, so in the summer standing up too fast meant risking having the flesh torn from my legs.

The mall was a magical place to a youngster in the 1980s. Mom would take Seth and I to McDonald's and buy us Happy Meals, spending $1.99 on Seth's Hamburger Happy Meal and $2.09 on my Chicken McNugget Happy Meal, and she would buy herself a Big Mac and Fries. Our Happy Meals would be served to us in brightly colored, barn-shaped paperboard boxes, which often contained jokes printed on the side panels and featured punch out sections that were themed with the toy prize. Mom always chose which yellow plastic booth we sat in, careful not to sit too close to the smoking section. We sat in the booth happily eating our aptly named Happy Meal food and reveling in amazement at whatever prize McDonald's happened to be giving out that week. Over the years I amassed quite a collection of Happy Meal toys, ranging from Berenstein Bears with flocked fur to Lego bricks to glow-in-the-dark Halloween buckets to Transformer-style robots cleverly disguised as McDonald's food. After the meal was over we would throw out the mostly Styrofoam trash in the tan and brown garbage cans, although sometimes I would keep the Happy Meal box.

After McDonald's we would head to the Fun Factory, an arcade that was full of video games and some traditional favorites like pinball, crane machines, and Skee ball. The cool thing about the Fun Factory was that the arcade games spewed out bright orange tickets that could be traded in for prizes. My excitement would build as I stepped into the arcade and the juke box blasted out all the latest songs like "Walking on Sunshine" by Katrina and the Waves, Bill Medley and Jennifer Warnes "I've Had the Time of My Life" from *Dirty Dancing* (which Mom refused to let me watch no matter how much I begged and pleaded) and Jefferson Starship's "Nothing's Gonna Stop Us Now." The songs from the juke box shook the air and were punctuated with the electronic beeping and bleeping eight-bit video games, and lights from the games flashed with hyperactive fun. Mom would give us our allotment of one dollar bills to put into the token machine which gave us four brass colored tokens for every dollar we put in. One of my favorite games was called "Bear Crane Mountain." One token would buy thirty seconds of time to operate a crane that would fetch as many toys as I could scoop up. I would typically get about twelve or thirteen toys in one game, usually key chains, tops, jumping frogs, and other small plastic toys. I grew quite adept with that crane game, and once on a different crane game in the arcade I won a white plastic Max Headroom mug with a matching yellow plastic lid. When I wasn't playing crane games I played the other games such as "Whack-a-Mole," and Skee ball trying to win as many tickets as I could in anticipation of the best part of visiting the arcade: The Prize Counter. The gleaming glass counter seemed to stretch for miles with countless varieties of wealth such as puffy stickers, jelly bracelets, cool pencils, plastic fish, fake monster fingers, fake insects (which Seth and I would leave on Mom and Dad's pillows to try to scare them), glow-in-the-dark spider rings, slider puzzles, mini-erasers, neon fabric bracelets, and those little popping UFOs that were clear neon plastic that you turned inside out and set on the floor and waited for a few seconds until they would leap up a foot and a half into the air. If you were able to earn a higher amount of tickets you could get things like small stuffed animals, notebooks in cool shapes, fruit scented plastic pencils with stacking lead points, puzzle balls, Chinese yoyos, and whoopee cushions which were fun to hide under the couch cushions when we had company. When I walked out of the arcade my heart over-flowed with joy because of my newly acquired prizes. I used to save the cardboard box from my Happy Meal if I knew I was going to the arcade, because this served as a convenient container to carry my numerous arcade treasures home in.

But as grand as the Fun Factory was, Kay Bee's toy store was another source of absolute euphoria. In the 1980s toy stores were spectacular places that were packed full of pieces of popular culture phenomenon such as handheld LCD video games, Cabbage Patch Kids, Simon, Pound Puppies, Rubik's Cubes, Koosh Balls, Weebles, Makit Bakit kits, Zaks, Poochie, Rainbow Brite, Duncan Yoyos, My Little Pony, Wacky Wall Walkers, Pogo Balls, Colorforms, Spokey Dokies, Lite-Brites, plastic Slinkies, Strawberry Shortcake dolls, Popples, windup toys, Neon Leons, Pee-Wee Herman action figures, Madballs, Laser Tag, Photon Guns, Domino Rally, Shrinky Dinks, and Barbie® dolls with big blonde hair-dos complete with curly or crimped hair that seemed to defy the laws of gravity (which looked quite impressive on an 11 ½ inch doll). They also made Michael Jackson dolls and sold clothing for them, so my Ken doll had the red "leather" outfit just like the one Michael wore in the "Thriller" video and it even came with a silver glove, which was actually a mitten since Ken's little plastic fingers were molded together. The shelves of toy stores were lined with toys from companies like Kenner, Tyco, Ohio Art, Ideal, Galoob, AmToy, Acclaim, and Coleco. It was here that I would enjoy the fruits of my labor by spending my allowance. Seth typically bought Micro Machines (from Galoob!) or Hot Wheels cars, and I usually opted for Pound Puppy Newborns, smaller versions of Pound Puppies that cost two or three dollars. One cool thing about those little puppies was that they were the perfect size to be dressed up in Ken's t-shirts. Pound Puppy Newborns didn't come in boxes, rather, they were strung up above the aisle by sharp metal hooks that were suspended on a long string (I couldn't help but think that it was kind of cruel to shish cabob the poor little puppies like that). I remember craning my little neck trying to decide which Pound Puppy I wanted, but because Mom stands less than five feet two inches she was too short to reach up and get me the chosen puppy. This meant I had to go to the counter and ask one of the clerks to assist me. I remember the thrill I felt when my purchasing power meant that a grown-up man (who, in hind sight was probably only about seventeen-years-old) would have to leave the counter to get me whatever puppy I wanted. The idea that I could have an effect on at least one grown-up's actions and make them do my will was quite enthralling.

I was always happy to walk into Kay Bee's, but leaving the toy store brought a sense of gloom and sadness. True, I did have a new toy in one hand and a Happy Meal box loaded with Fun Factory prizes in the other. But Mom, after spending her time and money making Seth and I happy would want ten minutes for herself to go and look at the clothes in one particular shop. The nerve of her! For me this was agonizing. At that stage in my life I didn't really like to shop for clothing very much and the concept of enjoying this fashion ritual was far beyond the realm of my comprehension. I only liked to shop for clothes if it meant I was going to get something neat to wear to school for the start of the year and that boring store didn't even sell kids' clothes so they didn't have any merchandise I was interested in.

I remember slowly trudging into the store with a feeling of defeat and despair. A bratty outburst of protest would have been unthinkable because if I had attempted it I would have gotten in a huge amount of trouble. At this time the floor of that particular store was covered in thick, hot pink shag carpet. One day I was so overcome with the grief of being trapped in a store I didn't like I couldn't even hold my head up, but this led to a fascinating realization. The shag carpet generously draped itself over the edges of my high top sneakers and I knew instantly that the monstrous looking carpet must be capable of generating a horrific amount of static electricity. I remember the feeling of joy and elation that swept over me as I dragged my feet across the carpet and headed towards my little brother who was facing the opposite direction, completely oblivious to the fact that I was accumulating a near-lethal amount of electricity. I was wondering just how powerful this new weapon was and was delighted to hear the loud *SNAP* when I touched his arm. Seth looked startled as he wheeled around and said, "Hey! M-" but just as he was about to tattle on me he realized that he was capable of vengeance. I scooted off in the opposite direction, shuffling my feet the entire way to "recharge" as I tried to avoid getting zapped by my brother. We happily spent the rest of our time in that store getting into what we would later call a "Shock War," dragging our feet across the carpet and playing an electrically charged game of Tag.

110

We did our best to subdue our laughter to avoid having Mom make us stand still and behave like normal human beings. The greatest moment of this particular Shock War was when Seth decided he would no longer run. He bravely stood his ground as I gleefully charged toward him. Seeing that he was not moving, I decided to test the level of his will power. I stopped right in front of him, and stretched out my hand, zeroing in on the tip of his nose. I cackled with delight at the creative direction my plot had taken. Time seemed to stand still. Seth stood there, daring me to challenge his courage. We stared each other down as I zapped the end of his nose. A loud *SNAP* sounded and, amazingly, a spark flew. It was a triumphant moment. Seth's reaction was laughter.

I have to say that I had a whole new respect for my younger brother for having the courage to laugh in the face of an electrical attack. When we left the store that day, we both walked a little bit taller. Of course, the fact that we were walking taller could be attributed to the static electricity making our hair stand up on end, but I prefer to think it was because Seth had demonstrated courage, and I had proven my creativity in the realm of sibling torment.

Creating a Not So Natural Disaster

I clearly remember the day that I discovered the miracle of carbonation. In those days, 12 ounce sodas came in glass bottles with Styrofoam labels that were really fun to peel off the bottle. The big two liters were plastic and at that point in history still had a round plastic base glued to the bottom of the bottle, and a metal cap to seal the top. I remember once when I was about five I was curious to see if the metal cap would float so I dropped it into Mom's glass (at least I was smart enough not to put it in mine). I was pleased that the little shiny metallic cap floated contentedly on the carbonated waves that the impact of the landing had created. Mom was reading a magazine and didn't notice, so I let it in there curious to see if it would stay afloat, which it did. I just sat there and watched it bob in the bubbles, waiting so I could warn Mom not drink it whenever she decided to reach for the amber colored drinking glass. For some reason I watched the cap, which now seemed like a little toy boat, with hypnotic interest. I'm not sure how long it took until Mom finally noticed it. She asked me why I dropped the cap in her drink and I answered her with a shrug. Mom carefully explained to me that I should never put a foreign object in anyone's food or drink, including my own, because it could cause a person to choke. The talk must have hit home because I've never since put a foreign object into any sort food or drink again, with the exception of those plastic ice cubes with fake flies in the middle (I outgrew that phase at about fifteen years of age – yes I know I was a troublemaker but it was such fun!). Mom wasn't mad at me for the cap floating incident, but she wasn't very happy that she had to waste a perfectly good cup of soda by pouring it down the drain and getting a fresh glass.

My greatest soda related memory of childhood happened one day when I was about six or seven. Mom came into the kitchen through the back door carrying a brand new two-liter bottle of a major brand of lemon lime soda. Before she had a chance to put the soda in the refrigerator the telephone rang and she hurried out to the living room to answer it because this was before we had an extension phone in the kitchen, a cordless phone, or an answering machine. This also left me alone in the kitchen with the gigantic bottle of soda. As a child I was curious about everything and that's a quality I've never outgrown. I readily admit that my love of books and learning probably borders on Obsessive Compulsive Disorder but since it's fun I'm not seeking treatment.

For some reason I was fascinated by all the bubbles in the bottle. I had seen soda a million times before so why this particular bottle intrigued me so much is not something I can really answer. Whatever the reason, I remember staring intently at the little bubbles through the green plastic bottle and watched them shimmy and shake and shoot upwards in a manic race to the top. I remember tapping the side of the bottle with my finger and watching as one lone liberated bubble flew to

114

freedom. I reveled in my power to manipulate the environment of the inside of the soda bottle. I grabbed the top of the bottle and shifted it off to the side, watching bubbles move and splatter and pop. It was totally radical! I lifted the bottle off the table and gave it one shake. The bubbles went wild and I was inspired. Since the plastic tan phone had Mom conveniently tethered in the living room I was out of her field of vision and I decided it was time to see just how many bubbles could be formed in one bottle of soda. This time I gave the bottle a harder shake. Bubbles were multiplying! I held the bottle up over my head and shook it as hard as I could. Somehow even more bubbles appeared! Once again I hoisted the bottle over my head and it was my turn to go wild. I paced back and forth across the kitchen swinging and shaking the barrel sized bottle of soda pop as hard as I could. When I finally stopped the soda had more or less turned into foam. I was delighted, but now bored. I set the bottle back down where Mom had put it when she first came in.

Naturally I wanted to drink some of the soda, and so I drug a wooden chair across the linoleum floor so I could reach the cupboard to get my treasured plastic Max Headroom mug – the symbol of my arcade victory. Mom had finished her phone conversation and came back into the kitchen. I heard a loud, roaring *WHOOSH* and turned around to see the most beautiful sight that I had ever seen! The bottle of what was once ordinary soda was now transformed into a beautiful, flowing fountain that was spraying the sparkling, sugary soda several feet into the air in graceful arches! It was like a magical volcano spewing liquefied diamonds! The joy! The wonder! To this day I can't recall that marvelous scene without having Tchaikovsky's "Waltz of the Flowers" from the Nutcracker Suite run through my brunette head. It was so spectacular that I'm surprised that a fairy godmother didn't appear because she would have had made quite an entrance against the beautiful background of bubbling bliss. But the splendor and the great beauty were about to come to a tragic end. Once the spraying soda subsided, which had even hit the ceiling much to my delight, Mom was nearly screaming in shock. "Oh! Oh! Oh my! What happened!?! All I did was open it!"

I vaguely wondered if my bubble experiment was in any way attached to the incredible display of wonder I had just witnessed. Quite timidly I said, "Um, um well, I shook it just a little bit."

"How much is 'a little bit'?" Mom questioned while she arched an eyebrow.

"Well just a little tiny bit. But then I shook it like this," I said while I ever so slightly moved my hands above my head and gently moved them back and forth.

"Why?" Mom asked in her loud question tone, which meant I might have done something to have gotten myself in trouble.

"I . . . I . . . I . . . well, I just wanted to see the bubbles go really fast."

"Did you know that if you shake soda it explodes when you open it?" Mom questioned.

"No," I answered truthfully.

"Well, now you know not to shake the soda next time," she said in a calm tone of voice, but I knew she meant business. Mom cleaned the kitchen and I couldn't believe that I didn't get into trouble. But perhaps the most amazing fact of the aftermath of the incident was that there was a tiny little bit of soda left in the bottom of the bottle. Mom shared what was left of the now severely carbonated beverage with me, which was very gracious of her, because if any woman ever deserved a soda, it was her after she got done cleaning up that nightmarish mess.

The Mysterious White Envelope

It doesn't seem like years and years have passed since the afternoon my teacher stood before me with a white legal-sized envelope in her hand. "Jade, I want you to put this letter in your backpack right away and make sure your mother gets it this afternoon.   It's very important."

"What is it?" I asked cautiously.

"Just make sure your mother reads it today," she answered in a stern tone.

I didn't have the slightest clue what was in that envelope but I could tell that it was obviously something crucial. I began to take a rapid mental inventory of my recent behavior and couldn't remember doing anything so heinous that would deserve a note home. But I never could tell. This was the same teacher who sent me home with a report card full of all the fantastic grades that I had earned but called my Mom in for a parent-teacher conference because she thought that I didn't like math (no, I'm not joking). When Mom went in for the conference the teacher disgustedly and matter-of-factly informed Mom, "I don't think Jade likes math." Mom told the teacher that she made sure that I did my homework every night and asked if I was handing it in. The teacher confirmed that yes, I did hand in my homework. Mom then asked if I had a bad attitude about math class or if I was giving her a hard time. The teacher said no, I was not demonstrating any problems with attitude or behavior.

At this point Mom was beginning to believe all of my previous claims that the teacher didn't like me. Mom asked, "Is Jade paying attention in class?" The teacher acknowledged that I did pay attention in class. Mom, thinking back to my stellar report card asked the big question to try to shoot down any doubts my teacher had about me asked, "What is Jade's grade in math class?" Mom already knew the answer thanks to my report card, and I wonder if she used the same loud question voice with my teacher that she used with me.

"Jade's carrying a 95%," the teacher answered.

"So what exactly is the problem if my daughter has an 'A+', pays attention, hands in all her assignments and behaves?" Mom questioned skeptically.

"I just don't think she likes math!" The teacher answered in an exasperated tone.

Mom never did understand why I deserved a negative conference. She left with the impression that it might not have been an issue of me disliking math (and truth be told I have never really cared for math) so much of it being an issue of the teacher disliking me. Mom was guessing it must have been some sort of a personality conflict, but she found the very idea that someone might not adore her daughter incomprehensible. The teacher having a bad attitude towards me during the conference was no surprise to me, I was quite certain she didn't like me, but at my young age I couldn't figure out why. Years later I was content to chalk the whole thing up as a personality conflict, but then I realized this wasn't very likely because I had a personality and the teacher didn't. So I'm still not sure why my teacher disliked me.

So, armed with the above knowledge is it any wonder that I was somewhat disturbed by that white envelope? The teacher must have seen my concern because she said firmly, "It's nothing bad." I was skeptical. None of the other kids were getting letters sent home. Fortunately the teacher had the sense to wait until close to the end of the day to unleash the White Envelope of Terror on me. I didn't believe her claims that it wasn't bad news, and I knew it wasn't good news either. Not giving it to Mom wouldn't be an option because I'm sure that my teacher would somehow find out about it and the teacher would subject me to consequences that no human being would ever want to face. The principal's office? Missing a week's worth of recess? Getting paddled? I certainly didn't figure that Mom would open that letter to find:

Dear Mrs. Heasley,

In an attempt to raise the school's budget for office supplies and stationary, we are sending random letters home. This will allow us to honestly say that we use up lots of paper and envelopes and the school district should be allotted more money for its operating costs. There is nothing to report, but we need to run the budget up so that we can buy more equipment for the school next year.

You don't need to take any action in regards to this letter, but please expect a minor tax hike.

Thank you.

I remember the frustrating feeling of suspense as I put the letter alongside my Trapper Keeper in my bright red Mickey and Minnie Mouse backpack. What was in that letter? What could possibly be so crucial that was neither good nor bad? I knew that whatever was in that envelope must surely spell out my doom. The suspense was almost too much for a poor, defenseless seven-year-old girl to bear.

Since Mom went through my backpack every night I didn't bother to tell her about the envelope. I decided it would be best to let her be surprised. I knew she would find it so I went about my afternoon trying to enjoy the time I had left of life as I knew it before the contents of the envelope were discovered and would alter the course of my existence. "What's this?" Mom asked as she pulled the envelope out of my back pack after dinner.

I rapidly blurted out, "I don't know, but the teacher said to give it to you and that's it's nothing bad." I think I was trying to reassure myself more than anything.

Mom casually tore the envelope open and I was relieved that it merely contained relatively harmless looking letter. I was somewhat reassured that it wasn't top secret government microfilm or something else along those lines. Her calm and relaxed demeanor made me think that perhaps whatever the letter was communicating wasn't something earth shattering after all, but that delusion was about to be blown apart.

"Oh," Mom said in a mournful tone, "you need glasses."

"I NEED *WHAT*!?" I half yelled in shock, furious at my teacher whom I was now convinced was aligned in some grand conspiracy against me. She said it was nothing bad! How could getting glasses be considered, "nothing bad"!?!

"You need glasses," Mom repeated sympathetically. My mind flew back to the mandatory vision tests we had to take at school. At the time it didn't seem like any big deal. Just how long ago was it? Weeks? Days? My mind was reeling. I failed a vision test and no one bothered to tell me? Shouldn't that be illegal? It could be a hazard! What if I had fallen down a flight of stairs and cracked my head open because I couldn't see where I was going? Or what if I would have stepped out in the road into the path of a tractor trailer that I never saw coming? I could have been flattened and my big plastic earrings would have been the only thing left to identify me with.

I thought about how the few bespectacled girls at school all seemed to wear similar blue plastic glasses and I was not anxious to join their near-sighted ranks. "I'm not wearing glasses! I don't need stupid glasses!" I insisted.

"Yes, you will be wearing glasses if you need them," Mom said gently but firmly.

I suddenly realized that my fight to keep my face lens free was a lost cause. It was a bitter, brutal defeat that would forever leave me disillusioned and left me perpetually suspicious of any authority figure who failed to give me a straight answer when I asked for one.

I remember the drudgery I felt in the long days in between the loathsome letter and my eye appointment. I lamented to my Uncle Shawn that I didn't want to get glasses because I was afraid I'd look dumb. The sixteen-

123

year-old sagely said, "I know a guy who didn't want to wear glasses, you could just do what he did."

"What?" I asked, hoping to hear that there was an alternative to being condemned to a life of corrective lenses.

"They make prescription sunglasses. Just get a pair of mirrored shades. That way instead of just looking like a little kid wearing glasses you'll like all those cool rock stars on MTV."

Mirrored shades. They sounded so cool! True, I had never seen Cyndi Lauper, Gloria Estefan, or anyone from the Bangles or Heart wear mirrored shades but I thought that mirrored shades might make me look really cool. One thing was for sure: rock stars weren't wearing giant plastic eye glasses. *Mirrored shades!* I treasured this newfound wisdom that my Uncle Shawn, who usually picked on me, had given to me. It would be several years until I realized that he was setting me up. Shawn knew dang well that mirrored shades weren't going to fly with Mom.

The only good thing about having to go for the eye exam at an actual eye doctor and to pick out frames was the fact that it got me out of school for an afternoon. The eye appointment went smoothly enough, but going to order my glasses was more time consuming than I had imagined. When I went into the room that had seemingly hundreds of thousands of pairs of glasses to pick from I was astounded. I had no idea that I would have so many choices. Mom said that I could pick out any pair of glasses that I wanted. That's when I made my official announcement, "Good. I want mirrored shades," I proclaimed boldly and walked over to the display of plastic sunglasses with lenses that had a high-polished mirror shine.

"You are not getting a pair of mirrored shades," Mom insisted.

"Yes I am. You told me I could pick any pair that I wanted and I pick mirrored shades." I thought I had her trapped in a technicality and I could smell victory amid the plastic of the thousands of pairs of over-sized glasses that covered the wood paneled walls. I was really starting to lean towards the sunglasses with plastic frames and had blue, mirrored lenses.

"Why in the world would you want a pair of mirrored shades?" She was getting that authoritative tone in her voice, and I knew that the next two or three sentences that I uttered would be critical to my winning the Great Eye Wear Debate of 1988.

I answered logically, "Because I would look cool. Then I wouldn't look like I was wearing glasses. It would just look I was wearing sunglasses."

"Don't you think you would look silly wearing sunglasses inside?" She tried to reason with me, but I wasn't going to give up so easily.

"I wouldn't look silly, I would look cool," I said.

"No you wouldn't. Nobody looks cool wearing sunglasses inside."

"Yes they do. Rock stars and blind people wear them inside all the time," I said, but then realized that I should have left blind people out of it.

"First of all, you can be glad that you're not blind." I could rapidly feel myself losing. Without giving me time to think of a response she said, "You are not hiding your big, beautiful brown eyes behind a pair of mirrored sunglasses."

"Fine . . ." I moaned. I knew I had lost. In my seven-year-old mind I couldn't help but wonder if I had scrunchy little ugly eyes if I would be allowed to have mirrored shades. I began to look at all the eyeglasses and made up my mind right away that I wouldn't be getting blue glasses, and I wouldn't get the ugly gold-tone aviators that were scaled down to look more feminine. To me they still looked like man glasses. I also ruled out the large plastic glasses that had the arms attached near the bottom of the lenses instead of near the top. So after trying on about forty different pair I finally found a semi-tolerable pair of glasses. They were pink plastic and in my mind they looked really nice, well, for as nice as glasses could possibly look. My new eyewear had a stylish, contemporary flair and looked a lot like Sally Jessy Raphael's glasses except they were pink instead of red. Mom decided that I should get plastic lenses instead of glass because they would be safer. I also had the option of tinting the lenses amber, but I opted not to because there were a few kids at school who had tinted lenses and I thought it looked like they had dirty faces like Pigpen from the Charlie Brown cartoons. Only grownups could get away with tinted glasses. I was convinced that my glasses were the prettiest that glasses could possibly be.

But looking back at those glasses, although child-sized as well as very in style, they were a humongous monstrosity that dwarfed my head. But nearly all kids who wore glasses in this era shared this same plight so at least I didn't look terribly out of place. This was a time in history before the days of ultra-thin lenses, and my lenses were really thick, not to mention that each lens was about six inches wide. I wore those glasses for five years until I got a pair of green metal marbleized frames in seventh grade. But I happen to wonder if my pink glasses didn't cause, or at least contribute to, some permanent side effects. On my Dad's side of the family all of the women are very tall. I only grew to be 5'4", which makes me the shortest bloodline Heasley woman in five generations (and possibly more), and the shortest known Heasley woman in three centuries! Yikes! That is quite an interesting family record to hold. Now you could say that it was genetically possible for me to be short since Mom is less than 5'2". But I wonder if wearing such big thick glasses, huge, heavy plastic earrings, and having a very thick and very long side ponytail didn't make me so top heavy that it permanently stunted my growth. I have to wonder. Perhaps you may find this suggestion ludicrous, but I think there is some genuine validity to this idea. But regardless, being short doesn't bother me like it once did. I take comfort in the fact that short people make the best entertainers. Don't believe me? Judy Garland was 4'11 ½", Mickey Rooney was 5'3", Natalie Wood was 5', James Dean was 5'7", Karen Carpenter was 5'4" and all of those 125 little Munchkins in *The Wizard of Oz* ranged from 2'3" to 4'8."

Think about it.

Taking the "Fun" Out of Fundraising

       Every child in America whose parents have ever let them outside of the house to see the light of day (as opposed to locking them in the basement to keep them from being corrupted by society) will be involved in some sort of fundraiser before they turn seven. I attended a public school, played soccer for three years, and was in Brownies and Junior Girl Scouts.

       One undeniable truth about these organizations is that they need money. The adults who ran these various organizations during my childhood either didn't seek the help of a kindhearted philanthropist or apply for government grants to help us out financially, or perhaps they did seek and were rejected, like poor little starving war orphans thrown out into the freezing cold of a snowy night. Whatever the case may be this left the old reliable route of fundraising to cure us of our financial woes. Certain items that school districts need stretch the budget beyond the allotment of cash provided by tax payers, sports teams need uniforms and equipment, and if Girl Scouts want to do something besides sit still in metal folding chairs and stare at the fake wood paneled walls, they need Popsicle sticks to glue together. Popsicle sticks and Elmer's Glue cost money.

Besides every girl bringing fifty cents in dues every week, Girl Scouts sold Girl Scout Cookies. This was the easiest fundraiser that I have ever participated in. I can't complain about selling Girl Scout Cookies, by the 1980s they were so well established that all I had to do was wave a paper in the air with pictures of Girl Scout Cookies on it and everyone within in a two mile radius was tripping over each other to place their order. I have to say that they are good cookies, especially if you buy Thin Mints and put them in the freezer for awhile. During the mid-1980s we sold the cookies for $2.50 a box. I was shocked, and quite pleased, that by the time I was in college fifteen years later the price had only gone up to $3.00 a box. I never thought I would see the day when a gallon of gasoline cost almost as much as a box of Girl Scout Cookies. My only regret with selling Girl Scout Cookies was that I never achieved the rank of Cookie Queen like my Aunt Kelly had done when she was in Girl Scouts.

When I was in Brownies I always wondered why we were referred to as "Brownies." How in the world did they come up with that name? Looking back, shouldn't we have been called, "Cookies"?

Based on the success of Girl Scout Cookies why can't every organization come up with one brilliant product that they can become famous for? This isn't the case, unfortunately, and doing fundraisers for school and soccer were entirely different endeavors. We'd be given threatening speeches that were disguised as pep talks about how the fate of the organization was in our youthful hands and that the failure of each one of us to sell less than

$250,000 worth of potholders would cause our fine group to sink in the quicksand of financial ruin, never to reemerge. But at only $17 a potholder, we only had to sell 14,706 potholders each to make over our goal. A mere 14,706 pot holders per child! Sure, people could go to Hills' Department Store and buy two potholders for $1.99, but this was for a good cause, and we were assured that the finest quality merchandise in America was not available in retail stores, but only offered to the public through a few privileged children who had the character and integrity to belong to a superior organization such as ours. We were given careful lectures about how our parents would surely dip into their savings account and take out a second mortgage on the house to support our group, and then we could nag all of our neighbors, relatives and our parents co-workers and friends who would buy extraordinary amounts for themselves as well as buy them to give as gifts. Hooray! Nothing says "Happy Birthday!" like a potholder!

Besides over-priced pot holders, I spent my childhood selling other shoddy merchandise such as ugly home décor, wrapping paper with foil printing that was guaranteed to not lose its color despite the depletion of the Ozone layer, and imported cashews in elegant tins, but the scary part was that no one knew where the nuts were imported from.

The companies who sold these goods knew that the futures of their companies really were in the hands of small children, because the junk they offered would never sell if it had to sit on a store shelf in plain view of the buying public. But if you had recruited a cute little six-year-old with big a big smile, showing off her newly missing front tooth, people would feel obligated to help out. But the only problem is that cute little six-year-olds are more business savvy than people assume. The thoughts of uniforms and equipment weren't going to be enough to make us surrender our precious free time for the sake of a fundraiser, which was about as much fun as drying the dishes or pulling weeds. So to bribe us into to doing their bidding these companies made sure every fundraising catalogue included a crucial element: The Prize Brochure. These were filled with the things that every child dreams of, such as giant doll houses, remote control cars, color televisions, and even official Nintendo Entertainment Systems! If you would only sell enough items you had your pick of the goods that would make you feel like some altruistic leprechaun had given you the treasure trove at the rainbow's end. Some of the more elaborate prize brochures had to be hoaxes, though. I remember one prize brochure promised that the first child to sell three million units would get the grand prize of their very own Las Vegas casino, complete with flashing neon signs and slot machines. If you sold fifty additional items, you would even have a semi-decent Elvis impersonator under contract for three years.

But for most of us, the thought of earning our very own Nintendo Entertainment System was enough to make us want to do everything in our power to sell everything in the catalogue one hundred times over. I remember asking Mom to buy things, which she always did. No matter how expensive or worthless the product might be, she could be counted on to do her part to help me out as well as whatever fine organization was using her underage child as a sales clerk. Family members and Mom's friends could usually be counted on to buy at least one thing from me, Uncle Jim never once turned down the opportunity to buy at least one item, and sometimes Aunt

Kelly would buy two, or even three items! Dad would take the brochure to work, too. I remember one time I was looking through one of the 50,000 fundraising catalogues I had as a kid and was excited to see that they sold sets of tools. Since Dad was a mechanic I was certain that he would want to buy one, and I figured that the car dealership he worked for would want to buy enough for every mechanic that they had on staff. So I was crushed when Dad told me that he wouldn't be buying any tools because they were generic. But looking back I have to say that Dad more than made up for it because he usually ordered an abundant amount of Girl Scout Cookies, so besides getting credit for the orders I also got to help eat the cookies. Who says you can't have your cake and it eat it too? Or in this case, cookies. By my second year of selling Girl Scout Cookies I learned that it was best to give the order form to Dad before Mom had made her final decision, because Dad would buy four boxes of cookies instead of two like Mom did.

When I look back at my childhood fundraising attempts, no matter how hard I worked I just couldn't ever get close to earning the Nintendo Entertainment System, or the giant doll house, or whatever else in the prize brochure had caught my eye. I would usually end up with something from the first or second prize group out of about six levels of prize groups. About the only prize that I can clearly remember being truly excited over was a giant set of markers that I had earned in school fundraiser when I was in kindergarten. They came in a thin, blue plastic holder in the shape of a paint palette. There were probably eighteen or twenty generic markers, some in exotic colors like pink or gray that weren't the typical marker colors at that point in art history. There were even different shades of blues and greens. I had a lot of fun with the marker set for about two days until all the markers dried up. I was sad about it because I always put the caps back on them. The one other prize I can remember is a nylon wallet with a Velcro closure. It was my reward for selling eighteen items for a soccer fundraiser. I picked it out of the prize brochure and didn't give much thought to the small print under the picture, *colors may vary*, so I was kind of disappointed that the wallet I received was camouflage. Somehow it just didn't seem to go well with any of my little toy purses.

But looking back I have to say that the practical skill of learning how to sell people stuff that they wouldn't ordinarily buy did come in quite handy since I would spend the first few years of my early adult life going to college by day and working retail at night. I never would have guessed that even at the age of five I was beginning to train for my first career.

But come to think of it, I started printing at the age of two so I guess I began training for my career as a writer during my toddler years.

Television Like You've Never Experienced Before or Since

Cartoons in the 1980s were probably some of the best cartoons in American history. During the week there were *The Littles*, *The Jetsons*, *Richie Rich*, *The Get-along Gang*, *Ducktales*, *Chip and Dale Rescue Rangers*, *Inspector Gadget*, *The Noozles*, *Heathcliff*, *Alvin & the Chipmunks*, *Shirt Tales*, *Danger Mouse*, *Maple Town*, and *The World of David the Gnome*. Although it wasn't technically a cartoon, *Fraggle Rock* deserves a place of honor in the 1980s Kids' TV Shows Hall of Fame.

Another contender for The 1980s Kids' TV Shows Hall of Fame is PBS's *SquareOne*. Although this show had a lot of neat music video and skit segments, the ultimate part of that show was Mathnet, a *Dragnet* parody that featured Mathematician/Detective Sergeant Kate Monday and Mathematician/Detective George Frankly. Let me take this opportunity to say that Kate Monday was one of my childhood heroes and I watched *SquareOne* every afternoon. The most suspenseful episodes were the two that almost resulted in the deaths of Kate and George. George almost got killed after hiding in a stolen car that got crushed, and Kate was almost blown up by her psychotic neighbor because she had learned of his bank-robbing ways while she was stuck in a wheel chair because of a leg injury. Although the purpose of the show was to teach kids mathematical skills, I studied Mathnet with great intensity because to me it was like getting free detective lessons. Mathnet was fantastic to watch, how else could you possibly get kids interested in learning mathematical concepts developed by 14th century Italian mathematicians? Remember the parrot Little Louie who recited the first few digits of the Fibonacci sequence? All throughout the 1980s Mathnet was really exciting with all kinds of plot twists and turns. Even into the year 1990 it was still cool. But one horrible day in 1990 Kate disappeared and never came back. She was never seen or even heard from again. She was replaced by Pat Tuesday but the show was never the same. Still, I kept watching Mathnet.

But for those of us who were children in the 1980s Kate's disappearance was unnerving and we didn't forget that she had been there. It resulted in an endless string of unanswered questions and we never learned her fate. I find it ironic that the greatest mystery of Mathnet went unsolved. What happened to her? Did she decide to go back to L.A. after she and George were transferred to New York City? No, too simple. That would have been acknowledged. Certainly she couldn't have disappeared as the result of foul play because George would have desperately tried to find her. Besides, all of us loyal little Mathnetters knew that Kate was too sharp and too smart to fall prey to criminals. But even ruling out certain things didn't answer our questions. I'm guessing she went undercover.

During the latter half of my childhood my dream was to work for the F.B.I. and so any TV show that was about spies or detectives had my attention (as long it wasn't a scary show for grownups like *Unsolved Mysteries*). I was certain that if the government would only hire me and train me as a spy that I would be the perfect secret agent. After all, who would suspect that a short little nine-year-old girl with huge glasses would be a brilliant international spy? Besides, maybe if I was a spy I would be able to have a computer book just like Penny on *Inspector Gadget*.

However, the above mentioned shows were classics, and as incredible as they were to watch during the week, Saturday morning was a fantastic time to sit in front of the TV and watch hours of cartoons as well as live action classics. These amazing shows included: *Pee-Wee's Playhouse*, *Muppet Babies*, *Teenage Mutant Ninja Turtles*, *Garfield and Friends*, *The Smurfs*, *Pound Puppies*, *Snorks*, *Popeye and Son*, *The Flying House*, *Teen Wolf*, *The Adventures of Raggedy Ann and Andy*, *The New Adventures of Winnie the Pooh*, *Mighty Mouse*, *Super Book*, and *Hey, Vern! It's Ernest!*

I wonder how many kids in the 1980s would, if given the choice, have picked visiting Pee-Wee's Playhouse over Disney World. When I was six I saw the film *Pee-Wee's Big Adventure* and wanted Pee-Wee's bike for Christmas. My Mom told me that Pee-Wee's bike wasn't a real bike that could be purchased at a store (It wasn't for sale, Francis!); it was a special bike made just for the movie. I figured that since they already made the movie they didn't need the bike anymore and that maybe Santa Claus could fly his sleigh into the movie studio and get me the bike and leave it next to the tree (although I never could figure out why Pee-Wee left his playhouse on a ho-hum scooter instead of his awesome bike). I couldn't think of reason why I couldn't have Pee-Wee's bike. After all I was a very well-behaved little girl. Most of the time.

The idea of having a bike that could fly was awesome. I thought that I could ride it to school and when class got boring I could leave my classroom and ride off on my flying bike and not have to go to school for the rest of the day. It's not like the teacher or principal could catch me if I was several hundred feet in the air. I guess it never occurred to me that if I showed up at home several hours early that Mom would make me go back to school and apologize. But needless to say I didn't get Pee-Wee's bike. It was a depressing day to learn that the bike couldn't really fly – it was just some movie special effects. It was the same sad story for the really cool flying surfboard he had in *Back to the Beach*.

I used television as a reference point for planning the numerous successful careers I wanted to have as an adult such as spy and detective (Mathnet), robot builder (*Short Circuit*), treasure hunter (*The Goonies*), and rock star (The Bangles' video of "Walk Like an Egyptian"). Although they weren't inspired by television other careers I was determined to have were that of scientist, inventor, and artist. I also wanted to become an author, and work at the Crayola crayon factory so I could invent new crayon colors and give them names. I wanted to be as rich as Scrooge McDuck and have my own money bin to swim around in. I wanted to be a mother and I was also determined to be the first woman President of the United States.

I had two other dream careers planned out from a very early age. One of the earliest career ambitions I can remember having was to be a Queen. I always played Queen, but I never played princess. From what I could gather from the story books that Mom had read to me, all that a princess did was sit around and stare out the window and wait for the prince to arrive. Even at that he usually didn't show up until after she found herself in some sort of life-threatening peril that she couldn't get out of on her own. But the idea of being a queen was far more appealing because she had already married the handsome prince, who was now ruling beside her instead of off fighting dragons in a foreign land. She also got to make all the laws and boss everyone around and if anyone got on her nerves she could lock them up in a dungeon, which sounded like fun to me! But the best part was that she could sit around in a big room filled with gold treasures and play with jewelry all day. Looking back that was a relatively well-developed thought process for a four-year-old. I used to play Queen Jade by sitting on the throne I had made out of a cardboard box and had decorated with the most elegant crayon scrawls I could muster. I would put the cardboard throne right in front of Mom's chifforobe so I could pretend that my throne stretched ten feet into the air. I sat on my throne in a Burger King Crown, weighed down with twelve pounds of costume jewelry given to me by Aunt Kelly and Gram Harman, and presided over my imaginary kingdom. My political skills must have been good because I don't ever remember my kingdom going to war. I understood why lands ruled by kings were called "kingdoms" but I couldn't figure out why lands that were ruled by queens were also called "kingdoms" instead of "queendoms."

For awhile I also wanted to be a lady pirate captain because this would be another opportunity to boss people around and wear lots of jewelry. Besides, I could live on a boat and have my own island, and the idea of owning my own beach complete with buried treasure appealed to me. My cardboard throne also served as my captain seat for my imaginary pirate ship, a doll cradle, and as the seat in my imaginary rocket ship when I played astronaut. Inspired by Sally Ride, I also wanted to be an astronaut when I grew up. I thought that astronauts were amazing and that they probably had better adventures than anyone else. I dreamed of flying through the stars and walking on the moon. But when I was in Kindergarten the *Challenger* came to its tragic end and it really shook me up. I was convinced that if I became an astronaut that I would get blown up, too. My dream of being an astronaut ended as soon as I saw the horrible footage on the news.

Of all the various career ambitions I had as a child, I have achieved one: writer. I suppose one out of fifteen isn't bad, all things considered.

But as great as the kid's shows were, primetime television in the 1980s was far more innocent and family themed than it would later become. I remember watching *The Muppet Show*, *Punky Brewster* (I had an amazing, multi-colored pair of suede Punky Brewster high top sneakers in first grade), *Silver Spoons*, *Mama's Family*, *The Facts of Life*, *Perfect Strangers*, *Family Ties*, *Webster*, *ALF*, *Growing Pains*, *Who's the Boss*, *The Cosby Show*, and *Full House*. I feel bad for young families now-a-days because they don't have nearly as many options for family friendly programming that everyone can watch. But that wasn't the case in the 1980s (for the most part). There were some shows that Mom and Dad wouldn't let me watch, but there were plenty of shows that I could watch. I remember that I was allowed to watch *The Golden Girls* until I made the mistake of telling Mom that I thought it was funny to hear old ladies swear. She didn't let me watch that show after that and I didn't see it again until I went away to college.

One of my favorite primetime shows was *Full House*. I remember watching the show thinking that D.J. had the coolest clothes, and wishing I could I could get my hair to look like hers. My naturally curly hair just couldn't ever be styled in quite the same way that D.J.'s was, but since the 1980s were a time of humongous hair-dos having out of control curly hair worked. But the main reason I watched *Full House* can be summed up in two words: Jesse Katsopolis. I thought that he was so handsome! John Stamos was the first celebrity I ever had a crush on (unless you count the boy who break danced in the Chef Boyardee Tic-Tac-Toes commercial, but he wasn't really a celebrity in the traditional sense). I remember it seemed like all the girls at school and in my Girl Scout Troop would have endless conversations about which New Kid on the Block was the best looking, but I never really engaged in any of those debates because Jesse was the man that had my attention during that time (but if you want my opinion I thought that Joey McIntire was the cutest of the New Kids). I remember telling Mom that I was disappointed that they had written Becky Donaldson into the show, but she said not to worry because John Stamos wasn't married in real life and that made me feel a lot better. Now that I'm an adult and have seen numerous reruns of *Full House* I have to say that even at the tender age of nine I did have discerning eyes for good looking guys.

The 1980s were a time of awesome cartoons, music videos, television shows, feature films, and made-for-TV movies. Every artistic medium that embraced the motion picture camera was turning out some great work. As if we Americans weren't flourishing in this area on our own, Canada presented *Anne of Green Gables* to the world in 1985, starring Megan Follows and featuring Jonathan Crombie, Schuyler Grant, Colleen Dewhurst, and Richard

Farnsworth. Mom and I watched that movie together quite a bit, a luxury that was afforded to us by the VCR. I remember being impressed by it for multiple reasons, the first one being that I couldn't imagine that PBS would ever show any program that would interest me that didn't feature puppets bursting into song every few minutes. *Anne of Green Gables* was the first "grownup" movie that I ever took an interest in. Secondly, it was Canadian. I didn't know that they made movies or TV shows in Canada (keep in mind I was only five or six) and I was impressed by my first foreign film. I have to say that watching Anne (spelled with an "e") shatter a slate on Gilbert's head was shocking, but also pretty cool. I had to admire Anne for sticking up for herself, but Gilbert was so handsome I didn't understand why she couldn't give up her grudge born of a vegetable-related insult and be Gilbert's girlfriend. I was glad that she finally came to her senses, but I was totally puzzled at the end of the movie when he called her "Carrots" again after he had endured years of crawling back into her good graces. Why would he go and do a dumb thing like that? For some reason Anne didn't get mad the second time, but maybe she just didn't happen to have a slate handy. It took me a few more years of life experience until I finally understood the last scene of the film. Even though the last few minutes of the movie left me confused as a kid, the rest of it was outstanding. Telling off a rude old lady, accidentally intoxicating Diana (and let's face it, Anne didn't force feed Diana three tumblers of wine), a mouse drowning in pudding, scaring Aunt Josephine half to death and then mocking her frightened reaction behind her back were all fun things to watch. But what I think I admired most about Anne was her determination and intelligence. It was pretty neat to see a child that knew as many big words as a grownup and could outsmart everyone at school.

One thing that I never noticed about the 1980s until after they were over was the fact that it was the golden era of elderly crime solving sleuths. There was Andy Griffith in *Matlock*, Angela Lansbury in *Murder, She Wrote*, and Tom Bosley in *Father Dowling Mysteries*. There was also a string of Perry Mason (who was by then a senior citizen) made-for-TV movies. It's interesting to note that this trend of shows starring aged entertainers seems to have been kicked off by a woman who was feigning old age – Vicki Lawrence. She created her famous Mama character at the age twenty four for *The Carol Burnett Show*. Vicki's sharp-witted senior citizen character would go on to enjoy a long run on her own show, *Mama's Family*. It's not unheard of for women to claim that they are years younger than they truly are, but Vicki Lawrence added years to her age with a gray wig and granny glasses to become the star of her own sitcom. Interestingly, Rue McClanahan and Betty White started out on the original *Mama's Family* and ended up starring in *The Golden Girls*, which featured Estelle Getty adding years to her age with a gray wig and glasses. Both shows were hits. I should note that it wasn't only primetime television that became a senior citizen (or pseudo senior citizen) super stardom launching pad, advertisements were a popular star-making vehicle as well. One of the most unforgettable commercials of the decade featured an elderly lady twisted into a pretzel knot and unable to move after an unexpected tumble, making, "I've fallen and I can't get up!" a national catchphrase.

And people bash American culture for being so youth oriented and overlooking the elderly.

143

The Secret I Buried in the Sandbox

When Seth was little he had a sandbox that we always had lots of fun playing in. He had some shovels and buckets, a sifter and a few other sand toys that he kept in it. I remember one evening I was out in the backyard playing and I came across one of Seth's many G.I. Joe action figures. Typically Seth kept all his G.I. Joe men and vehicles in his room, so how this one lone warrior ended up in the sandbox alone is a mystery. Maybe Seth took a bunch of them outside to play and forgot to take this particular one back in the house. I picked up G.I. Joe and realized that he had more working joints than an actual human being. How did they get a toy made from hard plastic that was so small to be so flexible? I was curious as to how G.I. Joe could be contorted in so many different ways. I realized that it was possible to twist G.I. Joe's torso the whole way around. I was curious as to how this was possible and pulled G.I. Joe apart slightly and was surprised to see that he was held together by a rubber band. I twisted him around a few times and when I let go of his legs he twisted around and around in a wild spasm. *Cool*, I thought. I wanted to see this incredible feat again, it looked like in addition to being an excellent soldier G.I. Joe had mastered the fine art of break dancing. I twisted

145

G.I. Joe up again but this time something terrible and unexpected happened. I apparently wound the rubber band too tightly because I heard one quick and horrible *SNAP!* I had accidentally broken G.I. Joe in half! I instantly knew that I was going to be in a massive amount of trouble if I didn't come up with a plan in a hurry.

I quickly looked at the house, my eyes scanning over the enclosed back porch and all of the back windows of the house. I was relieved that no one was there and no one had seen the destruction I had caused to what seemed to be an indestructible action figure. I did the only thing I could think to do. I dug a deep hole in the sand and carefully placed G.I. Joe in it and covered the hole over. I never breathed a word about it to anyone and managed to escape the punishment I feared I would be receiving.

Nearly twenty years later, after Seth and I were both adults, he said to me, "Do you remember that big bucket of Legos you had as a kid?"

"Yeah," I smiled as my mind drifted back to the countless afternoons I spent digging through hundreds of Lego bricks looking for the one specific piece that was needed for whatever project I happened to be working on that day. I'll never forget the sound the plastic blocks made as I raked through them sorting them out.

"You know how you had those little red flowers that came with that house set you had?" he asked.

I nodded, "Yeah, but they seemed to disappear fairly soon after I got them." I was never quite sure what had happened to them.

Seth chuckled, "Well, I have a confession to make. I used to think they were really fun to chew."

"You *chewed* Legos?" I asked in shock. "How in the world did you manage to do that without tearing your gums to shreds?"

"They weren't hard plastic like regular Legos, they were made out of some other type of plastic. Anyway, one day I spit one out in my hand and it was all chewed up and flattened out and I realized that there was no way it would ever fit back on any of the Legos. I knew I was going to get in trouble for it if anyone found out so I just chewed it up really good and swallowed it."

"Seth . . ." I said as I laughed in disbelief, "is that what happened to all of them?"

He was laughing too, "Yeah," he answered.

"I remember when they all started disappearing and I had this theory that they were so tiny that they bounced out of the bucket and fell in the cracks on the stairs," I explained.

Seth shrugged and said, "Sorry, but I ate them."

I couldn't help but laugh, but thinking back to childhood I recalled the G.I. Joe incident. "That's alright, but while we're on the subject of confessing about breaking each other's toys, I accidentally snapped one of your G.I. Joe's in half once."

He scrunched his eyebrows as though he was beginning to have a faint recollection. I said, "I was out in your sandbox once and I found a G.I. Joe and I twisted his legs all around just to watch him spin and I managed to snap the rubber band. I knew I was going to get in huge trouble so I dug a hole and hid him."

"I remember that! I was digging through the sandbox one day and found him split in two. I just looked at him and thought 'I don't remember doing that.'"

I shrugged, "It was me. Sorry." I tried to keep from laughing.

Seth just grinned, "Whatever. I guess maybe I had it coming for chewing up your Legos."

"Well, at least I gave G.I. Joe an honorable burial," I offered.

The Newsstand

Just around the corner from our house sat our town's newsstand and candy shop. I remember the many sunny days that Mom would walk there with Seth and I, and she would give us each a quarter. A quarter! You could get a lot with a quarter in the 1980s, a choice of a Hug drink, a pack of Garbage Pail Kids, a Ring Pop, a Lik-m-Aid Fun Dip, a box of Nerds, a bag of Middleswarth Chips, a pack of Pop Rocks, or any combination of cheap candy. A dime would give you your pick of: a pack of Sixlets, Bottle Caps, a Tootsie Pop, a small Peppermint Patty, a candy necklace, a candy watch, a box of Candy Cigarettes, or a Whistle Pop. But perhaps the most fun was buying penny candy. There was a row of plastic bins that held the candy. Now that we live in an age of anti-bacterial hand sanitizer it's kind of funny, not to mention disgusting, to think that every kid in town stuck their grubby hands in containers of unwrapped candy but back then we never gave it a thought. We children marveled at the parade of plastic bins containing red Swedish fish, purple Swedish fish, hard candy strawberries, Frooties (the Tropical Punch flavor was the best), Tootsie Rolls, bubble gum cigarettes, generic Pixy Stix in plastic tubes, and Pal Bubble Gum. I would usually pick a combination of Swedish Fish, strawberries, Frooties, Tootsie Rolls, generic

Pixy Stix, gum cigarettes, and usually one or two pieces of Pal. I used to love to "smoke" the bubble gum cigarettes and watch the cloud of powdered sugar puff out the end of the cigarette. It always made me feel like a rebel and a grownup. These gum cigarettes are getting harder and harder to find because some people feel that they send a pro-tobacco message to kids. I bought bubble gum cigarettes all the time as a kid and can honestly say that I have never even tried a real cigarette so apparently the gum cigarettes aren't as influential as people think. Either that or I have extraordinary intelligence. I prefer to think it's a combination of the two.

If I wasn't going to be spending my money on junk food I usually went for one of two items: Garbage Pail Kids, or a toy plane. Garbage Pail Kids need no introduction to the true 1980s child; they were gross, disgusting, and completely irresistible. Aunt Kelly got me my first pack of Garbage Pail Kids when I was about five. Kelly has always been a very generous person and for the first several years of my childhood she would bring me some sort of treat literally every time she saw me, usually candy or gum, but one day she decided to get me a package of Garbage Pail Kids and without realizing it she brought me face to face with one of the biggest fads of the 1980s. The fact that adults were repulsed at the sight of cartoon snot and vomit were what made these trading cards so fun. Truthfully some of the more extreme cards did gross me out but since grownups were sickened by them I always kept the cards around. I used to love to go up to unsuspecting adults and happily say, "Look!" and show them a picture of a cartoon kid spewing a long string of snot and using it as a jump rope or doing something as equally appalling. This was especially fun if it was close to meal time. I spent several years collecting the cards and acquired quite the collection of Garbage Pail Kids.

The other fun thing to buy were those little balsa plane kits that you could put together yourself. But this was a luxury that required a little more money than a quarter. They came in a flat paper package for 79¢ and required carefully sliding the paper thin balsa pieces together to assemble the plane. This took great patience because if I wasn't careful, I could split the whole thing apart. Seth and I used to buy them, put them together and fly them in the living room. Mom would allow us to throw them in the big double living room of our Victorian era home. Normally Mom wasn't a big fan of throwing things in the house, but she knew that if the planes crashed they weren't capable of causing any harm to anything except themselves. The thick nylon carpet (another symbol of the 1980s middle class) provided a relatively safe landing. If we were really careful we might get the planes to make four or five successful flights before they crashed and broke. A few years went by and the newsstand started to carry another type of plane that was Styrofoam and preprinted in all kinds of cool colors. You could pick out different styles and they even came with little blue plastic propellers. At the low, low bargain price of 25¢ we bought these often. Sometimes we could fly them for two days before they crashed into a wall and were permanently bent out of shape.

Once I was old enough to cross the street by myself and Mom trusted me to be able to go on short errands alone, there were three places I was allowed to go and all were within 100 feet of our house. The first was to my Gram Harman's house, the second was the newsstand, and the third was the town library. Gram's was my

151

favorite place. My Gram thought that each one of her grandkids hung the moon and she always made us feel like we had made her day by stopping by for a visit. She always welcomed me with open arms and a glass of Kool-Aid. Gram was always full of love and encouragement.

When I wasn't heading off to Gram's or the newsstand I was on my way to the public library. I was in awe at the seemingly endless shelf upon shelf and stack upon stack of books. As a kid it seemed like there must have been four or five million books at the library. For me it was incredible to think that the answer to almost anything you ever wanted to know could be found in that one building. I remember that a lot of the shelves near the center of the library were about four feet high, and on the top of these shelves were small metal easels that were used to display books. I remember I had two favorite sets of books that I loved to read, one was the *Wayside School* series which had a lot of offbeat humor, something that I have always been a huge fan of. The other major 1980s series of books was *Choose Your Own Adventure*. I loved those books and read every single one I could get my hands on.

The other types of books that I read were history books. You may be thinking, *History books? You voluntarily read history books?* Yes I did. I read history books and sat in the library's reference room thumbing through the pages of the *Civil War Journal*, a hobby I began when I was seven or eight. By the time I was eight I could name all the U.S. Presidents forwards and backwards, middle names included. Not a typical childhood hobby, I admit, but what can I say? My love of history turned out to be a lifelong thing because when I grew up I earned a B.A. in History.

However, reading paid off big when I was a kid. I remember the BOOK-IT! program that was in place in my elementary school. If you read a certain required number of books in a month you could get a certificate for a personal pan pizza from Pizza Hut and a gold star sticker for the BOOK-IT! pins that were handed out in school. These pins were quite the popular item to be sported on jean jackets, at least in my neighborhood. BOOK-IT! pins were usually displayed next to the green and white "Just Say No" pins. I remember going to Pizza Hut in the late 1980s and enjoying the reward for my efforts. I always ordered a Personal Pan Pizza with pepperoni, and I noticed that the servers always made it a point to congratulate me on reaching my BOOK IT! goal. I always felt like a little celebrity. Looking back I have to say that getting rewarded with great food for making myself smarter, and getting a gold star sticker on my BOOK-IT! pin was a lot of fun.

Goodbye, Bessie

One of the tell-tale signs that the 1980s were drawing to a close (at least at our house), was on the night in 1989 that Dad decided to let me in on a secret. He told me that the next morning he was going to call Mom and tell her that he needed her to come to the car dealership where he worked. Dad had bought Mom a brand new car and wanted to surprise her with it. I was thrilled! A new car! He said for me to not let on like I knew anything, and to act surprised and disappointed that I had to have my day interrupted by having to take the one-and-a-half hour round trip to his workplace. Dad suggested it might be a good idea for me to whine about having to make the trip so Mom wouldn't get suspicious. Dad said that he wanted to do something nice for Mom since Mom was always doing nice things for other people.

The next day every time the phone rang I bubbled with excitement but managed to just act like there was nothing special about the phone call I was expecting Mom to get. Seth and I were sitting on the floor of our double living room playing with Lego bricks when the phone rang. I heard Mom ask, "Are you serious?" "How much is that going to cost?" "Is insurance going to cover that?" "Can't you take care of it yourself?" Once the phone call was over Mom said to us, "Kids, just to let you know we've got to go get your Dad from work later on this afternoon. When he was driving to work this morning he was driving behind a truck that was hauling rocks and one fell off and bounced up and punctured the radiator of his car."

This was my cue. It was the only time in my life that I had permission to whine and I fully intended to run with it for all it was worth. "Aw," I whined, "I don't want to go."

"I'm sorry, Jade, but we very well can't let your Dad be stranded at work." Mom said.

"He's a mechanic, why can't he just fix his own car?" I mouthed off. I loved this legalized whining!

"Yeah?" Seth asked skeptically.

"I didn't plan on spending my afternoon like that either, but the shop doesn't have the type of tools he needs to repair it. He had to send it out to some place that specializes in radiators."

"Fine . . .," I muttered with a scowl, but inwardly I was really excited and couldn't wait to see the new car.

We made the trip down and I got out of the car and kept my excitement contained. When we reached the section of the shop where my Dad worked there was a brand new 1990 Honda Civic LX. The paint was a glossy white color and Dad was putting the finishing touches on the pin striping. The car had a giant red bow on the roof, it was about three feet wide and the elaborate loops stood a foot in the air. "Is that for me?" Mom joked.

Dad ignored Mom's question. He was acting completely casual like it was any other car. "Oh, some customer bought it to surprise his wife and he wanted me to pin stripe it."

"Wow," Mom was impressed. "Good for her."

Dad said, "Yeah, well fortunately for you I was the customer."

Mom was shocked and asked, "What!?"

Dad grinned and pulled a set of keys from his pocket. "It's your car," he said as he handed her the keys.

"How in the world did you manage to buy a new car without my finding out about it?" she asked, still stunned.

Dad shrugged and grinned, "Oh, I have my ways."

Mom got over her shock and started beaming. "I can't believe you got me a new car!" she said, and threw her arms around him.

Dad hugged her back but said, "Be careful you don't get your shirt greasy from my uniform."

"I don't care," Mom said, but somehow her shirt stayed clean.

Dad said, "So I guess you've probably figured out by now that my car's just fine. I just made the story up to get you down here."

Mom turned to Seth and I, who were anxiously peering through the windows of the new car. The interior was blue, and the fabric covered seats meant an end to the days of having my legs sticking to the seat in the summer. "Hey kids, guess what?" Dad began, "That car has air conditioning *and* a tape deck." Air conditioning and a tape deck! I couldn't have been happier. Bessie had a tape deck but she didn't have air conditioning.

"So are you surprised about the new car?" Mom asked.

"Yeah!" Seth said with a happy laugh.

"No!" I beamed; thrilled that Dad had let me in on the secret a day early.

"What do you mean 'no'?" she questioned.

"Jade knew about it. I told her," Dad said.

"You knew about this?" Mom asked and gave me a puzzled look.

"Don't act all surprised, you know Jade can keep a secret," Dad said.

"I know Jade can keep a secret, but you should have heard the way she was carrying on and complaining about having to ride down here," Mom said.

"Good, I told her to so you wouldn't be suspicious," Dad explained, and held up his hand for me to slap him five. It was nice to have my dramatic acting skills appreciated for the true asset that they were.

I remember making the forty-five minute trip home in the new car. I sat in the front seat because I "forgot" to call the front seat before we left the house, knowing that Seth would claim it if I didn't. At our house the rule was whoever called, "Front seat!" first meant that they got to ride in the front seat on the way to wherever it was we were going, and the other one got the front seat on the ride home. Now I was riding in the front seat on the way home in the new car, just like I had planned. Mom found another unplanned surprise concerning the car when we got home. Seth had managed to get a hold of a black pen and got some ink on the back seat, much to Mom's dismay.

Bessie the Station Wagon was left at the dealership for Dad to drive home, and Mom did have to run him back to work the next morning so he could drive his own car home after work. But since Mom got a new car out of the deal she didn't mind one bit. The sleek new little Honda that got 43 mpg was quite the change from the big old clunky station wagon. It was the dawn of a whole new era.

The Next Era of Video Game Technology

By the late 1980s the Nintendo Entertainment System became wildly popular. The Japanese two-toned gray video game console was the most amazingly high-tech piece of computerized wonder that I had ever seen. Uncle Shawn had one, and this was very much a repeat experience of his Atari because I wasn't allowed to touch the Nintendo, even though Gram tried to reason with him since I wouldn't hurt it (apparently he had forgotten about the Crack Jack revenge incident since he never brought that up to argue his case), after all I was nine-years-old by that point. Shawn always let my cousins Kasey and Jason play Nintendo and they weren't that much older than me, which added to my frustration. I remember one time when Shawn let me try playing *Super Mario Bros.* and gave the strict warning that I could play one game, and that was it. I knew the basics of the game and was thrilled when I finally got a turn. My cousin Erica had always let me play her Nintendo, but she lived on the other end of the state and I rarely got to see her. Finally, with Shawn's Nintendo controller in hand I began a game. Shawn decided that I needed help, so he would start giving me really loud advice. "JADE! LOOK OUT FOR THAT TURTLE! IT'S GOING TO KILL YOU! LOOK OUT! LOOK

OUT!" Of course having an eighteen-year-old scream at me from two feet away was distracting and I couldn't concentrate on the game, so Shawn's rotten plan to cause Mario's quick demise was always successful. Once I survived the turtle he would say things like, "YOU'LL NEVER MAKE IT OVER THAT HOLE! WHAT ARE YOU DOING GETTING A RUNNING START LIKE THAT!? YOU'RE JUST GOING TO RUN OVER THE EDGE! JUST GO THE EDGE AND JUMP AND HOLD DOWN THE ARROW KEY!" If you remember playing *Super Mario Bros.* you know that following those instructions will make Mario plunge to his death. My game usually lasted less than two minutes and ended with Shawn gleefully announcing, "Alright, give me the controller. You had your game."

My cousin Jason got a Nintendo for Christmas of 1989. Jason was my Uncle Keith's son. I always loved going over to Uncle Keith's, he had more record albums than most music stores and I thought that was really cool. Uncle Keith and my Aunt Izzie were always very nice to me and I have a lot of happy memories of playing games with their kids, Kasey, Jason, Lee, and Nicole. They had a huge yard that was the perfect place for Seth and I and our four cousins to play Wiffle Ball as well as Army and detectives. I had fun playing the games that the boys wanted to play, but I must confess that I would have liked to have gotten them to play Barbie® dolls from time to time. The idea of trying to get Kasey and Jason to play Barbie® dolls would have been unthinkable, because I had once made the suggestion and when they excitedly starting planning my doll's doom with explosives and gasoline I was horrified. Jason always shared his Nintendo with me although he almost always made me be Luigi. I have to say that once I actually got to play *Super Mario Bros.* without

Shawn screaming in my ear I didn't turn out to be too bad of a player. *Super Mario Bros.* and *Duck Hunt* were always fun, but Jason also had *Excite Bike* and *Paper Boy* which were really great games. Besides owning cool games, Jason also rented some different ones from time to time. By this point the video store and most of the other places in town that rented VCR tapes were now renting Nintendo tapes. Too bad they never did that with Atari cartridges.

Owning a Nintendo was not a part of my 1980s experience, but Seth and I got one for Easter of 1990, so it wasn't too long after the 1980s drew to a close that we finally had a Nintendo of our own. After five years of Atari (a span of time that was almost as long as Seth's entire life) we marveled at the Nintendo and couldn't believe just how realistic all the graphics were. Mario's facial features were mostly distinguishable and the green pipes looked 3-D. We fought over who was going to be Mario and who would be stuck having to be Luigi. Besides *Super Mario Bros.*, the Nintendo came with *Duck Hunt* and the official Nintendo Zapper. But perhaps the most wonderful thing about the Nintendo was that it had a "pause" button, and that brilliant addition meant that we could put down the video game controller long enough to go get a drink without having to worry about the electronic death of the video game character. Nintendo seemed to be the pinnacle of video game technology. How little did we realize that video games were still going to come a long way.

New Years Eve, 1990

On December 31, 1989 my Mom's family gathered at our house to usher in a new year and a new decade. Uncle Jim and Aunt Brenda were renovating their kitchen and so we were hosting our family's annual New Year's Eve bash. There was a lot of food, a big game of Trivial Pursuit underway and lots of chattering by twenty-some people. The youngest in attendance was my toddler cousin Tony, who was Uncle Shawn's son. Ever since Tony was born Shawn had been nice to me, with the exception of being a Nintendo Scrooge. Whether he decided to be nice to me in all other cases was because having a child had turned him into a mature adult or he was fearful that I could take my revenge for years upon years of torment by picking on his son, I can't say for sure. But I am sure that Tony, as well as his mother, my Aunt Laura, appreciated my profound maturity by letting bygones be bygones.

I was nine-years-old on that New Year's Eve and I remember thinking that an era was coming to an end. The 1980s were the only decade I had ever known and I had a strange feeling that something wonderful was going away forever. I wondered what was going to be different about the 1990s. I knew two things for sure: I would have two new cousins. My Aunt Kelly would give birth to a son named Blair seventeen days after that party had ended. Aunt Laura was pregnant with a little girl who would be named Natasha. A few more years into the 1990s Aunt Laura would have another daughter named Christen and Aunt Kelly would have a baby girl named Karman. I didn't know then that before the 1990s ended I would get two more cousins on Dad's side of the family, Aunt Cheryl would have a daughter named Katie and Aunt Patty would have a son named Miles.

I knew that I was going to graduate from high school during the 1990s but when you're in the fourth grade graduation seems a million years away. How was I to know then that before the 1990s were over my family would have moved to the other end of the state for four years, and then moved back home again? I didn't know that by the end of the 1990s I would be halfway through my sophomore year of a private college that had accepted me on a music scholarship, on that New Year's Eve I had never picked up an instrument. I had no clue that before the upcoming decade was out that people would be able to walk around with a working phone in one pocket and a computer in the other. I wouldn't have guessed that something called e-mail would make it possible to type a letter and send to someone else, and have them be able to read it instantly from almost anywhere in the world. Like many Americans, I had no idea that the internet existed or how quickly all sorts of information from anywhere in the world would right be at your finger tips. I don't think anyone who lived in the 1980s would ever have guessed that aerosol hairspray would largely become a thing of the past, or that almost all major fast food chains would stop using Styrofoam. I wonder if everything that radical environmentalists claim about the danger of Styrofoam containers is true. I would like to think that all of the

Styrofoam containers that I have eaten from will never biodegrade, rather they will exist continually in the soil as a testament to future centuries that I once walked this earth. Someday in ages to come when I am gone and the inscription on my tombstone is no longer legible, it is comforting to think that my fast food containers will endure and co-exist with the earth until the end of time. I sure hope so, anyway. But alas! My only regret was that I didn't write my name on them in permanent marker.

I could have scarcely imagined the wonders that the new millennium would bring. On that night in 1989 I would never have imagined that there would have be anything like an iPod, let alone that owning one would inspire me to write a book about the decade that was ending. Furthermore, I never would have dreamed that I would be writing that book on a laptop computer that could put Penny's computer book to shame. That New Year's Eve was an era when Seth and I would accuse each other of hogging the Atari and not taking turns, so I wouldn't have imagined that one day I would be teaching Seth's two beautiful daughters how to play the old video game classics on something called The Atari Flashback II.

Time marches on. Every decade will have its music, fads, fashion, movies, toys, television, and elements of popular culture to define it. Trends come and go and sometimes circle around again, but there will never be another decade like the 1980s. I can't imagine another decade I would have rather spent my childhood in. I'm sure that the majority of 1980s kids would agree with me.

10412513R00107

Made in the USA
Charleston, SC
02 December 2011